*Truth and Falsehood in Visual Images*

# Truth and Falsehood
# in Visual Images

————— Mark Roskill and David Carrier

The University of Massachusetts Press    Amherst, 1983

Copyright © 1983 by
The University of Massachusetts Press
All rights reserved
Printed in the United States of America
Library of Congress Cataloging in Publication Data
Roskill, Mark W., 1933–
Truth and falsehood in visual images.
Includes index.
1. Aesthetics. 2. Truthfulness and falsehood.
1. Carrier, David, 1944–  .  II. Title.
BH39.R67  1983     111'.85     83–5123
ISBN 0–87023–404–8
ISBN 0–87023–405–6 (pbk.)

# Contents

*Dedicated to the memory of E. C. H. R. (1904–1983)*

*Whatsoever things are true, . . . whatsoever things are lovely . . . think on these things.*   PHILIPPIANS 4:8

# Preface

THIS IS A PHILOSOPHICAL essay based on concrete examples.
Therefore it does not contain the detailed logical arguments
that might be expected of it within the field of aesthetics. We
find that version of aesthetics dull or overextended, and correspondingly think of this as a short book that may appeal to art
historians and philosophers interested in the choice of examples and their implications; to sociologists or anthropologists
concerned with the visual arts, including photography and
advertising; and, more generally, to all who are concerned with
the underlying premises of verbal and visual communication
and the relations between the two, to which we make frequent
reference.

We hope that the very form of the book may engage readers
of those differing kinds in stimulating and at the same time
serious ways. The illustrations are chosen from amongst the
many images or types of image referred to and are laid out with
such an appeal in mind.

We enter the field without any basic contention to offer as to
what makes a visual image true or false, or what it means
historically so to describe one. This is because there are two
distinct denotational frameworks that stand ready to entrap
one for definitional purposes. Both of them come up in separate
sections of Ernst Gombrich's *Art and Illusion*. He states in his
chapter "Truth and the Stereotype" that "a picture . . . can no
more be true or false than a statement can be blue or green";
which is a logical pronouncement about two-dimensional
images possessing some kind of informational content, which
usually have an identifying title or caption attached to them (on
the museum wall or on the page). Earlier, on the other hand, he
had used as epigraph to another of his chapters the passage
from Liotard's eighteenth-century treatise, "Painting can per-
suade through the most evident falsehoods that she is pure
Truth." This as an affirmation about the capacity of painting to
affect our beliefs belongs in a tradition of aesthetic and critical

response to the power of illusion in the arts in general. The problem from the beginning is not simply reconciling two such differing viewpoints, but dealing with the ambiguities—not to say confusion—that arise over their application in the contemporary world: one in which photography, advertising, and the development of modern art all have contributions to make to what is brought into account when truth and falsehood are being considered.

Briefly, we claim that visual images cannot be true or false in the sense that the propositions of science or mathematics are true or false, but that they can be considered true or false, or come to seem that way, in the varying senses in which we ascribe truth to an account of a significant historical event or of a person's behavior; to a document such as a will with a series of signatures on it; and to a perspective on social and political values held in a particular period or community. Put baldly, such a claim may seem obvious. But how visual images can be true or false in each of those senses and in what differing ways correspondingly particular images may lay claims to being considered true or false require considerable elucidation.

We start, accordingly, not with any absolute definition of what constitutes *a true* image, or makes for *the true* look of someone or something in a particular medium or style of representation, but with basic ways of conveying truth (what is meant in calling something true, what counts as true, what is held to be true). For a visual image to do this entails its communicating that suggestion, connotation, or implication, without any necessary truth of reference to a particular subject or object.

We have, then, a network of meanings gathering around the word *true*. Whatever questions we pose about the truth of pictures are related, certainly, to the variety of ways in which we talk about truth in everyday discussion, both with explicit reference to the appearance of things and in the more general way in which we say that statements or verbal presentations are true or false. Here obviously our interest in the truth of pictures relates to a more general debate, first about linguistic usage and then about philosophical reconstructions or revisions of that usage. Three examples of such usage would be: "I know a true patriot when I see one"; "This is the painting's true surface" (said during its cleaning); "There was a true balance of forces in Cromwellian England." The point is not so much whether the labels *true* and *false* do or do not apply, but how and on what basis they are arrived at. And in fact—to continue with the three-part form of exposition already adopted, which will be maintained for consistency and clarity throughout, though with variations as the discussion unfolds—there are three corresponding versions of visual truth.

First, an image may convey a certain truth about the world, in the same general way as a map or globe designates or denotes the fact that the world is round; convention-governed forms of representation do this as a matter of principle, within a prevailing schema of usage (as with stick figures). Second, it may communicate an accepted or ready-to-be-accepted truth, so that it constitutes evidence to that effect—as a photograph testifies that John F. Kennedy died of a gunshot wound: it puts into visual form what occurred, or serves as a marker of what transpired that day. Third, it may sum up and show forth what is held or found to be true about people and things; either in a general sort of way, as a cartoon or a calendar page may exemplify the proverbial truth that "a man's dog is his best friend"; or specifically for a time or place, as Aubrey Beardsley's drawings may be taken to show that he was a fop and liked foppish people.

Of course, someone might say that these were simply different meanings of the word *true*; that, if the word is thus inherently ambiguous, reconciling such different viewpoints is impossible and unnecessary. Photography suggests especially vividly why this facile answer is unconvincing. Compared with a painting, a photograph has in one respect a literal relation to what it depicts. A model stands before the camera, and what we see is her as she appeared through the camera. The photograph is, we say, true to life. But when that photograph is placed in the context of a Sunday supplement it may be false, we also say, in the way it links the model's beauty with the qualities of a perfume or motor car. The photo both truthfully depicts her and implies some false beliefs about these commodities. But though consideration of these ambiguities of truth in pictures may be thus nicely motivated by photography, there are questions that arise, also, in a more traditional art historical context. For example, if we follow John Berger's now famous account in *Ways of Seeing* we may want to identify a kind of essential falsehood in the whole tradition of European representations, photographed and painted, of women. We may attempt, with him, to juxtapose an Ingres odalisque and a modern pinup and note how both images imply a false or falsifying ideal of feminity. But can we really make such a comparison without misleadingly treating the Ingres as if it were just a pinup? More generally, how are questions about truth and falsity of photographs related to similar questions about paintings? This issue is one we will explore in some detail.

We have found it valuable to consider the viewpoints of the skeptic and the relativist, and the approaches of structuralist and Marxist writers, as they extend the terms of discussion. A brief introductory outline may be helpful here also.

The skeptic holds that any claim of truth is inherently dubitable. The painting claimed as a likeness of Holbein's may be a forgery; a photo may have been tampered with; the events depicted in a print may not have taken place (or at least not in that way). And so any pronouncements of truth that are put forward and upheld will be necessarily contingent ones. The relativist holds that claims to truth have validity only in relation to the circumstances, context, and situation in which they are made. A portrait of the sixteenth century may appear true in the light of the circumstances that produced it (such as the use of drawings from the life); a photo may appear true in the context of nineteenth- and twentieth-century conceptions of documentary accuracy; a print may appear true in the situation of its being the only record available of a historical incident, such as a hanging. But there are no more absolute and universal standards to go by, linking one age or one person's perspective on truth with another's.

The skeptic's case is not particularly challenging insofar as it rests only on the possibility of deception. We may indeed be misled, on the counts described, but unless the deception is deliberate and purposeful, in such a way as to make the image ambivalent, we are not necessarily bothered with respect to truth. One way of comparing the skeptic's claims to the relativist's is to contrast explicitly photographs that we speak of as "fabricated," and those that have been tampered with. Stalin might have had a photograph created showing Lenin embracing him and holding an angry fist under Trotsky's nose. Such a photograph would be a fabrication, since as a matter of historical fact we know that this was not Lenin's view of Trotsky and Stalin. Here our independently available knowledge of history serves to justify our belief that Stalin tampered with the authentic original image; tampering both makes this image literally false and implies a misleading view of the facts about the Revolution. Contrast that to one of John Heartfield's photomontages showing Hitler giving his salute and receiving in his raised hand money from a German capitalist. That image has obviously been tampered with—and we are meant to see that—but part of the goal of the artist was to create by tampering a truthful fabrication. To put the point in paradoxical terms: by obviously fabricating his image, Heartfield created a truthful statement about Hitler's backers. So a photograph or a painting may turn out to be staged, in the artificiality of its arranged components, and yet it may give an effect of truth that stays with us or even grows stronger. Here the viewpoint of the skeptic takes on greater interest: is the fact that a visual image can become more or less true a fact about the nature and character of visual images, or one that reflects the nature of our claims about them? Or is the distinction that is made by the second *or* here one that is, in fact, misplaced? Structuralism is valuable here for its focus on prevailing forms of language and their conventionalized character. In constructing claims about visual images and their history, we are *also* constructing claims in words about our perception of them: the point for the structuralist being to make the latter, and their workings, explicit.

The contention of the relativist differs from that of the skeptic in that it does not entail a commitment to any view, either positively or negatively directed, of what is consistently or existentially true. If the perception of truth in visual images is not simply a matter of each individual's personal inclination or liking in these things, then it would seem that any discourse about and around this subject must be contextually "framed." The importance given to that "frame" becomes, then, a historical or interpretative way of offsetting one's own. But the Marxist viewpoint, in its focus on forms of consciousness, sees in such "framing" the expression of social, political, and cultural interests shared between communities and classes. It thereby turns the concern of the relativist, that each period be considered in its own terms, back upon itself. How each culture and society articulates its sense of truth is to be seen reflected in its images, in the form of forces that are at work there to uphold the status quo or that struggle emergently against it.

One question much debated in contemporary philosophy is whether the position of the skeptic or relativist can be stated in a way that is not self-refuting. That debate is relevant to our present concern with pictures. To say that all statements are perhaps untrue, or that all statements are true only in some context, is to make claims that themselves aim for truth. But just as the logical positivist's claim that a statement is true if and only if empirically verifiable is itself false by that criterion, so a general statement of the skeptic's or relativist's claim falls into a similar trap. And here two interesting possibilities arise. First, perhaps we can get by with some limited notion of truth. Maybe *true* means only, "true for us," and we can recognize that at later times standards of truth will be revised in ways that for us as yet are unknowable or even unimaginable. After all, what we are concerned with is the use of images by our contemporary society. A critic, Philip G. Hamerton, wrote in 1863 that Manet's *Luncheon on the Grass* shows that "the nude, when painted by vulgar men, is inevitably indecent. Cabanel's *Venus*, though wanton and lascivious, is not in the least indecent. . . ." Perhaps in another century this claim will seem plausible again. In the meantime, it need not change our estimate of Manet's achievement. Second, there might be some way of talking about truth of pictures that escapes this problem of historicism. Perhaps, as Marxists imply, truth here is relative to an image's ability to show the class structure accurately; or, possibly—and this is a less sweeping claim—our privileged historical viewpoint gives us a way of knowing, better than earlier observers could, how truthful images—at least images from earlier times—are.

The versions of these arguments that we introduce are not treated as a basis for refutation or confirmation of a systematic sort, for, even supposing that to be possible, their helpfulness to the subject of visual truth does not require this. Rather, they are used to clarify the terms of our own discussion.

How we approach these issues is related to our different backgrounds—in academic art history (Roskill), in philosophical aesthetics (Carrier). Nowadays all readers of Foucault and Barthes know that "the author" is a fiction; that there are only texts. But this text has two "authors," Mark Roskill who wrote and revised the whole, and David Carrier, whose drafts on individual topics and comments on the successive revisions led toward this final text. The way this book was produced is responsible, then, for features of its structure. We are aware of how contemporary art historians are usually only marginally interested in questions of aesthetic theory; we know, too, that philosophers' treatment of such questions characteristically tends to have little feel for the complexity of actual art historical examples. Our goal, then, is to deal with art historical issues in ways that are philosophically sophisticated; and to point out how thinking about those issues may be a starting point toward what we regard as a most urgent task, the forging of a link between traditional art historical concerns and contemporary art. Considering here the nature of visual truth is, we think, a good way of opening debate about these issues. For "truth" is both a concept of central importance within philosophy and, as we now begin to see, a key notion in ongoing debates about the status of photographic images. To seek intellectual closure now, to offer a definitive or complete statement about these questions is certainly premature. What attracted us to this debate was, rather, the relation it bears to those ongoing concerns. Our text proposes some novel ideas, produces an array of examples, and offers some suggestions for further research. So this book represents a contribution to an ongoing debate, one in which we ourselves intend to continue to participate.

We would like to pay our respects to a number of people whose writings have given us a sense of how to proceed—even where we actively disagreed with them—and who have helped us also to identify the issues that we take up by correspondence or discussion: in particular, John Berger, Arthur Danto, Sir Ernst Gombrich, and Barbara Herrnstein Smith. For their interest, suggestions, and critical or editorial comment, we would also like to thank: Craig Harbison, Gareth Matthews, Alexander Nehamas, and Marianne Novy, and James S. Ackerman for introducing us to one another.
M.R./D.C., *March 1983*

# Chapter One

# On the Nature of a True Visual Image and How to Find One

*To the end that we may be true to our nature, we should not become false by copying and likening ourselves to the nature of another. . . . We should, instead, seek that truth which is not self-contradictory and two-faced so that it is true on one side, false on another.*

SAINT AUGUSTINE [1]

*Those masterful images because complete*
*Grew in pure mind, but out of what began?*

W. B. YEATS, "THE CIRCUS ANIMALS' DESERTION"

1. Gustave Courbet, *The Stonebreakers*, 1849–50. Formerly
Gemäldegalerie, Dresden, destroyed in World War II.

ASKED FOR A true visual image, what would one choose? One might reasonably think first of a picture such as Courbet's *Stonebreakers* (fig. 1). What then does it mean to speak of a painting such as this as true?

It might be taken—especially by art historians—that what this meant was an affirmation of the character of its subject matter and style, and a placing of it for this purpose according to a sliding scale of judgment that might include (for the modern period) the work of David and Delaroche—and also possibly Jules Breton's figures of farm workers and Degas's dancers. To adapt a remark of Stendhal's on Constable's rural scenery: while a freshly painted English millpond is all very well, one might expect art to offer something more physically impressive, more up-to-date, more enlightening, especially as time went on, and especially if one were Champfleury.[2]

But the judgment might be comparative in a narrower and more chronologically specific sense, as when contemporaries compared the *Stonebreakers* with Millet's *Sower*, shown also at the 1851 Salon in Paris, and found the latter a greater success in terms of "sentiment" or easier to come to terms with as representative of the new "realist" school, since it showed "a rude peasant—a countryman from head to foot."[3] In which case—as quite often occurs when what is "true" is equated with what appears convincingly "real"—one is making an assessment that involves the artist's way of working (in Millet's case, from memory and observation of the typical, rather than from detailed preliminary sketches) and characteristic emphases (on the shape of shoulders and legs with Millet, as opposed to clothes or ground underfoot), without implying any necessary correspondence with an actual person of that kind and appearance.

But it is also possible to take the painting as true to the physical and social implications of manual labor that give it its meaning, as Courbet affirmed was the case when he wrote of the picture (in 1849): "In these jobs this is how you begin and how you end up,"[4] and possible as well to claim that for this purpose—as Max Buchon put it in his 1850 advertisement for

Courbet's Dijon exhibition—Courbet did not need to exercise his imagination, he only had to show "a man who actually was in flesh and blood at Ornans as you see him," and in this way he could create a painting that remains "imperturbably sincere and faithful."[5]

Many socially minded critics since have affirmed this—echoing the view of Jules Vallès who said, when he saw it at the 1851 Salon, that this was recognizably a work that could "play its part in the triumph of justice and truth."[6] But because this large and finished picture has receded long since into history as a standard illustration in textbooks, and because it is known today only through reproductions (having been destroyed in World War II), so that the sheer physical impact that it had when seen in the flesh is no longer recoverable, perhaps this affirmation could still be regarded as a relative one. Since there are, in cases of this sort, so many different versions of a truth that is comparatively established, let us take three other images with very different claims to being true and consider those claims equally.

Toulouse-Lautrec's *Loie Fuller* (fig. 2) is a color lithograph which, with the addition only of lettering, might have served as the image for one of his posters. Loie Fuller danced using colored lights and transparent veils manipulated by rods, and one could say that the print is true to the way in which she performed and the way in which her dancing was experienced by the viewer, in its definition of the defiance of gravity and ballooning of organic shapes that the spectacle entailed. "Truth" here is not a matter of likeness (as in many portrait heads of Loie Fuller from this period) or of verisimilitude of behavior (as in statues showing her body and costume in motion),[7] which are the normal criteria in "correspondence" theories of truth, stressing (we may say) truth of representation.[8] Nor does calling the image "true" depend upon the clarity or convincingness of any prop or property shown, for it does not "look true" in that sense; the point being rather that it is felt (recognized or acknowledged) to encapsulate the character of Loie Fuller's dancing.

2. Henri de Toulouse-Lautrec, *Loie Fuller*, color lithograph, 1893. Smith College Museum of Art, Northampton, Massachusetts, Gift of Selma Irving ('27), 1978.

A photograph from the first moon landing (fig. 3), transmitted electronically back to earth, shows the American flag planted on the moon's surface. Plainly and straightforwardly it shows that. To suppose otherwise, to contend that it had in fact been taken in a cave in Kentucky would (if it were not satirical mischief) imply either paranoid delusion or an elaborate conspiracy theory. This is a true image, then, in attesting as it does that a flag was planted there, on that terrain, in conditions which would cause it not to flutter, to cast very distinct shadows, and so on. It does not depend for its truthfulness on being a composition of a deliberated and structurally articulated kind, as images do that, in accordance with "coherence" theories of truth, attain to truth of depiction (as we may call it) of a compelling kind.[9] One could say, indeed, that—unlike a nineteenth-century photograph of a lunatic grimacing under electric shock treatment, or a caricature of Churchill prowling the House of Commons—it was not necessarily designed to be compelling; and particularly so if (as with the more recent photographing of Saturn) its processing was computerized. For provided that it was still readable in its reconstituted form, what degree of such processing would render it noncompelling?[10]

Last, a woodblock illustration may be introduced, one which appeared in the *Illustrated London News* in February 1899 (fig. 4). Made from an artist's drawing, it shows a recent event that was presumably semispontaneous in character: the torchlight demonstration in honor of the Silver Wedding of the duke and duchess of Saxe-Coburg. For the contemporary or later viewer dealing with a graphic reconstruction (as the accompanying caption implies to this to be), truth here is a matter of the way in which features of ceremonial ritual and crowd responsiveness are brought out, of a kind appropriate— then as now—to royal occasions in Europe. The image does not need to draw for this purpose on what is known or assumed already about the situation arising presentationally and its codification in visual form, as is taken to be the case in "convention" theories of truth: these being ones that stress truth of

3. The American flag on the moon, photograph, July 20–21, 1969.

reference within an accepted scheme or system of notation.[11] It is reference to such a scheme or system that allows one to read Dürer's *Great Horse* in perspective, as occupying more space than the image appears to have room for, or to understand Mantegna's man on a slab with feet protruding as a foreshortened image of the dead Christ; whereas in news illustration, the technique used to give a sense of concrete detail and the combination of different elements brought together to convey what was to be seen are inherently more arbitrary.[12] One might compare from this point of view the way in which Flemish paintings of the fifteenth century (such as Memling's *Sorrows of the Virgin*), combine selective elements or episodes of a larger narrative whole within a common spatiotemporal setting. There, however, the larger sort of narrative "truth" that is thus generated is a matter of structural concatenations that are imposed on an existing story in an interpretive exten-

8

4. The Silver Wedding of the duke and duchess of Saxe-Coburg, torchlight demonstration at Schloss Friedenstein, from a sketch by artist Melton Prior, wood engraving, *Illustrated London News*, February 4, 1899.

sion of its logic. In the news illustration, the idea of a truth adhering to the artist's trained selectivity and insight into the character of the event, though it might be verifiable by reference to an independent printed account of what took place, is more likely to be taken on trust.

Having opened up these four images for discussion in this way, we shall not compare them with one another according to their degree of truthfulness; for if we juxtapose them in pairs or sets, as in traditional exercises of comparison in art history, we shall be tempted to do so according to the history of the medium (for example, its developing role as a repository of certain kinds of information), and its expressive potentials. To take this route would be to fall back onto a terminology that was brought into being for a familiar and useful but restrictive purpose with respect to truth: one devised to make it possible to categorize the achievement of artistic truthfulness as an evolving goal in each particular medium to which it can be made to apply, and, in some phases, even a dominant ambition.

What in contrast appears as more interesting in the choice of examples brought up is, first of all, how the same image can be considered both true and not true at different times. Unlike the case of the Courbet, for instance—where there will always be a large number of people (perhaps even a majority) who consider that Jules Breton's contemporary images of working people are "truer"—one can conceive of changes in the character of royal ceremonial taking place, such that the woodblock illustration was no longer considered "true" in the terms described. A contemporary analogy would be the way in which engagement photographs of the Prince and Princess of Wales invariably placed him on a slightly higher level than she, so that they presented themselves in a "match" and partnership in which his was the dominating, physically superior image. Should a time come when equality of the sexes became a live issue all the way up to the level of royalty, then one can readily see how images in which the prince appeared as the taller would give place to ones in which virtual parity of height between the pair was stressed. People would then be able to say a century later that the earlier presentation of the pair, untrue as it was to the facts (while not strictly falsifying them), was true to the prevailing male ideologies of the time.

A second freshly interesting point to emerge from the examples brought up is that a visual image may be charged with truth or untruth by virtue of what it comes to be recognized and acknowledged as being and that it retains the capacity to be so recognized and acknowledged irrespective of change in its physical appearance, such as the diminished clarity produced by reproduction of it or of alterations made to it as an organic entity (for example, by chopping down or trimming, or by the way in which the image is "framed"). The statement that the *Mona Lisa* represents a mysterious fantasy of womanhood does not forfeit its claim to validity when it is made in front of a very poor or badly cropped reproduction (or, for that matter, a colorless one); rather, just because the image is so famous and so ubiquitous, what is held to be true of the original in the Louvre becomes applied to its derivatives. By the same tokens, the statement made of the photograph referred to earlier of a grimacing lunatic, "There's the nineteenth-century idea of madness for you," does not lose its force of application if the version of the image that prompts it is in fact a much later reproduction in book form. Or to take a more practical example of what happens in the re-use of existing images, consider Andy Warhol's silk-screened repetition in his *Disaster* series (1963) of an electric chair from Sing Sing.[13] Granted this is verifiably and recognizably an image—complete with straps and a cord running up to it—of something that could still be seen and photographed (or had been open to being photographed not too long before), it remains that, even after Warhol has enlarged the image greatly, multiplied it many times over, bathed it in an overall tone of lavender or orange, and blurred parts of the image in the process so that it is much less distinct in its details.

The same also holds for the way in which an image may be charged with truth or untruth by virtue of how it is used in

relation to other images and thereby perceived. For example, a
particularly evocative photograph of the war in Vietnam may
be put into a larger collection of war photographs in such a way
as to bring out the special nature of that combat; or it might be
projected onto the backdrop of a theater performance. In the
latter case, once established in terms of its validity as an image
and the readability of what it shows, it can be commented upon
by what ensues in front of it, and even (if, for instance, it should
show the hero of the play dying shot) be endorsed or refuted in
its truth by the performance itself. An analogous example, in
the field of graphics and their demonstrative use, would be the
way in which the curve of a graph can be tailored, by means of
compression or a change of scale, to a particular argument or
mise en page.[14]

What then is the difference between our first example, the
Courbet (fig. 1)—or any painting, print, or poster that is comparably considered "true" in the Western tradition of artistic
development, because of the veracity of experience and the
grasp of material and social characteristics that it conveys (as in
the assessment of realism in the tradition of the novel)[15]—and
the second, third, and fourth examples (figs. 2–4), where the
sense of truth or untruth depends on what the images in question communicate, understood in terms of how they are generated, received, and understood over time? Record jackets, for
instance (to take a familiar and accessible example), may bring
back an image of the performer from an earlier cover or period
of his life, as being somehow representative—and continuing
to be—even though it no longer fits with his appearance or
current professional interest: as when portraits of Glenn
Gould, on reissues of his early Bach recordings, serve to
identify the time of first issue and to keep the youthful image of
him fresh, or when the cover of John Lennon's *Rock 'n' Roll*
(1975) depicts him as a leather-jacketed adolescent standing in
a slum doorway. The Toulouse-Lautrec lithograph, in fact,
could appear in a book to illustrate the expressive character of
dance movements, the moon photograph to document
American scientific "conquest" in the 1960s, the Silver
Wedding illustration to comment on royal wedding cere-

monial. The Courbet would not exactly serve in any of those ways, even for the subject of road construction in nineteenth-century France, unless it were so captioned or a significant detail was used for this purpose. Its place in book form would be, rather, to illustrate how proletarian labor and its conditions could be viewed in a certain way, as part and parcel of the development of Realist painting in the course of the nineteenth century. For all of its force of presentation, the character of its achievement with respect to truth seems curiously bound to its period or to circumstance in this way; and one wonders how to account for this.

There is a tradition in philosophy of questioning the grounds of human knowledge, one that, in the case of the arts, is based on the nature of the medium itself in which what is known or perceived is to be depicted or communicated. Since this form of questioning has been applied to both literature and the visual arts, the analogy between the two already brought up can be taken a little further here.

The tradition in point constitutes a form of skepticism inasmuch as it claims with respect to truth and falsehood that there is—can only be—what appears true from a certain viewpoint. Thus in everyday language and the framing of simple sentences, there will be variations of intonation, grammar, or usage governing the way in which ordinary words are used and affecting how they are heard; so how then can a basic or absolute meaning be attached to what a person says? Or in Nietzsche's somewhat playful version of this claim, since nature is infinite in the possibilities that it offers for its viewing and representing, it can only be represented by each individual in the perspective that that individual chooses to adopt; [16] and the knowledge of the world imparted from that viewpoint must necessarily be relative.

Two more sophisticated contemporary versions of these arguments are to be found in audience theory (applied to literature) and in structuralism (applied, in the version to be quoted, to painting). Both affirm the multi-valence of a work of art, such that any single determining interpretation or characterization of its nature becomes impossible. And both make it the basis of their systematic analysis as to how a work of art lays itself open to understanding that the identification of truth, in whatever form, is to be taken as grounded in comparative frameworks of assumption and in relativity of perception.

The truth [that a "standard story" stipulates, whether it be the press report of a marriage or the implicit claim in a novel of a character's existence] is not a matter of a special relationship [the story] bears to the world but of a special relationship it bears to the users.[17]

It is for the semiologist to conduct back to its deep ideological determinations the exigency of "truth" which reveals itself, intermittently, in the pictorial field, in various species and on various levels. . . .The question remains one of the nature, the status and the articulation of the "signs" by which the reading is informed and oriented, which the reading attempts or not to constitute . . . into a system.[18]

How does what is being claimed here apply to the determination of what constitutes a fiction?[19] Certainly, if I should begin talking about a visit to Freud's offices in Vienna or making a drawing or sketch-plan having to do with such a visit, there will be many clues or details—either internal (details of where Freud sat, how he looked, or where things were in relation to one another) or collateral (my age, background, and so on)— from which the attentive listener should be able to infer whether I am describing a personal experience, retailing someone else's, or making something up that has a logic or structural validity of its own.

Likewise, the man Dr. Sigmund Freud may appear in a work of fiction as a man of like appearances and habits, who hypnotizes Sherlock Holmes (as in Nicholas Meyer's *The Seven-Per-Cent Solution*); as a figure who acts compellingly as the real Freud would have done in such a situation (as in E. L. Doctorow's *Ragtime*); or as a practicing psychoanalyst whose treatment of a woman patient makes reference to published analyses and writings of the real Freud (as in D. M. Thomas's *The White Hotel*). And a visual equivalent to the effect of the presentation as a whole in such cases would be what happens in our response, should we be shown a photograph of Martin Luther King, Robert Kennedy, and Gus Hall embracing one another: even though each figure is both recognizable and convincing in his behavior, the image as a whole will be taken to be a fiction.

Yet one may also have a case like the account, in a popular World War II novel by Nevil Shute, of the king conducting an investiture at Buckingham Palace. When the hero is asked what the king said to him as he pinned the decoration on, his answer is that he said "Sorry to be so clumsy": a remark that appears so true of George VI and true to him in character that it can be regarded equally (and indifferently) as something that he actually did say, might have said, or said in a quite different context. And analogously, if I draw Freud's features recognizably, and then add an indication of upper body with the arm in a certain position, or if I cut out a photograph or print of his head and upper body and add an arm that is doing something (as John Heartfield did in his photomontages), response to what I do could take the form of its being said to be very true of Freud (or to Freud): true to the way in which he looked, or sat, or treated his followers. A book's cover design in which Freud appeared in a landscape setting, along with past and contemporary figures in the arts and sciences about whom he had written sympathetically, or one in which his head and shoulders and Baudelaire's were linked together (in order to convey that the intellectual bonds between them formed the topic of the book), however recognizable by the same criteria his basic appearance might be, would not earn that kind of response.

It follows from the discussion so far that the examples to be taken up will include visual images of all kinds, and not just the sorts of painting or print that people first bring to mind, and take account of, when truth in visual form is brought into question. Not all of those images will be representations of someone or something, or contain interpretative elements, in the sense of an implied interpretative stance toward their subject matter or particular features of it; and some of them will be neutral from the point of view of signification, rather than putting a complexion on what they show. A color patch of pink represents, at the most basic visual level, an example of an image that is non-representational and puts no interpretation on what it shows. It can be described and discussed according to its degree of pinkness, or its relative place within the color circle. But it can also be given signification by the context in which it appears, so that there will be a difference between how such a patch is viewed as it appears within a painting, such as one by Brice Marden, and how it is looked at in a box or a book of samples, when a redecoration is in process, or against the color of one's living-room rug.

The framework that will be used in what follows to address cases of the latter sort will be, correspondingly, more like that of the sociologist or the anthropologist than like that of the traditional art historian concerned with iconography or with symbolism. To amplify with an everyday example how such an approach turns on what may be called a "genetic" view as to the signification of visual images, rather than one that gives precedence to verbal or conceptual forms of ideation: a heart or the outline form of a cat carved on a rock surface would be an image that, in this approach, raised the question of why it was on *that* particular surface—in association with what other images—and how it, or they, got there. They could in their anonymity (as in cave art) be just elementary signs or markings, which then by a process of continuation and accretion took on a symbolic force; or they could be given the character of icons, as when the markings of weather on a mountain side turn into what comes to be seen as the features of a giant animal or of Lincoln.

To bring such cases into the discussion, furthermore, requires an understanding of what it means for an image to be a literal one, in the same general sense as George VI, the investing monarch in Shute's novel, appears there as literally himself. Common everyday examples of images that are literal would be shadows and footprints, which function as literal visual "traces" of the thing itself. But how a literal image is to be identified more generally, in and outside of a context that renders it symbolic,[20] requires further definition, and this is best done on an ad hoc basis. A print or a drawing, for instance, might include a blot or a thumb mark in it, which remains literally itself and is recognizable as such, while at the same time it has been incorporated into the design. A literal image in graphic form might be of a Greek temple facade (recognizable, perhaps, from the number of columns and shape of the pediment, as the Parthenon): one which appeared in that guise within a porthole form, against a ground of a consistent coloring, and possibly had writing attached to it.

The signification it took on would then derive from the character of that attached writing or the impress of the sign as a whole, as on the spine of the book. In either case, the writing could be said to adapt or to direct the use of the image, so as to give it that signification; and this is in fact a common pattern in the ways in which literal images are employed.[21]

The analogy in literature for extending the discussion to include such images would be to consider there not just truth in different forms of fiction, such as novels and love poetry, but also in those forms of writing (and speech) that can be considered either as special forms of literature or as functional appendages to the literary work: advertising jingles, promotional leaflets in their layout and typography, blurbs on the dust covers of books, disclaimers of resemblance to real and living persons at the front of novels, and so on. To do this makes it possible to move beyond the concerns of comparativist and relativist argument, inasmuch as the claims and professions present in such cases ask to be taken on their own authority: like a visual sign by the roadside that warns of snakes but does not need to specify how dangerous or poisonous the snakes might be. Such examples also open up the terms of discussion for truth and untruth, so that they become more interesting (there need not be any snakes there at the moment, or they may be quiescent, but the relevance of the warning to passers-by or picnickers is not affected by such considerations). A particularly suitable case to consider is that of the author's photograph as it appears on the jacket of a book, either in association with a biographical statement or independent of one. With or without such a text attached to it, the image here may vouchsafe, in the matter of truth, that the author is one who addresses him- or herself to the tasks undertaken in the book in a recognizably professional manner; or that he or she has traveled to the place that the book describes; or that he or she evinces as a person qualities of behavior or special interests that are appropriate to the book's subject. For instance, the portrait of Wayne Andersen that appears on the jacket of his *Gauguin's Paradise Lost* (1971) shows him as an outdoorsman with an Indian and bohemian look corresponding to Gauguin's image of himself; and that of Sherry Turkle on her *Psychoanalytic Politics: Freud's French Revolution* (1978) implies that she is a person with the sophistication appropriate to her topic. In Renaissance and Baroque publications, the portrait of an author printed to go with what he wrote could do the same only in a more discursive or indirect fashion, with greater weight given correspondingly to the import of the text.

Book jackets and record-cover presentations most often assign parallel roles to image and text in each part of their design, and this leads into the further question of how combinations of images (such as one frequently gets here) and descriptive sentences or passages differ from one another in affirmative force, even when they are mutually reinforcing. To go back to the example of rock carvings, the soldiers of the Spartan general Leonidas who were about to battle the Persians carved on the rock face of the pass an injunction addressed to the passer-by: "Go tell the Spartans . . . that we died for them." Placed there in advance of the battle itself, it would enable the truth that it recorded to be recognized subsequently. In this way the text comes to act as a marker of an inscribed kind, as on a gravestone or commemorative plaque. Analogously, two hearts together on a rock or tree become the affirmation of a particular couple's love for one another, at the time of making and proleptically thereafter. They *become* this when juxtaposed and integrated with other elements on the same surface or perhaps by a later addition, because the couple may have been the very first to do this here or have come back later to add more. The elements in question could be initials or words or a date, but there could also be other "signs" to which they become related.[22] The image of the two hearts thus designates the feelings that a certain couple (perhaps anonymous) had for one another at the time—though they may have proved false with time; it testifies to their having been at this spot; and it also affirms their adoption of a certain socially charged practice in this connection (perhaps one that was standard for engaged couples in that part of the world). In each of those respects there could be words that did the same thing, but they would not do so in exactly the same way. The nature of the difference here is most distinctively brought out by considering the role that a particular image plays in a sequence or series of images, as compared to the verbal indications given by a descriptive statement that follows and leads on to others. The truth of how a person changed between two periods in his life which is affirmed by the insertion of a certain photograph of him in a sequence of such photos might focus on the same features of his way of life and appearance as a verbal account, but it would not correspond in the provision of a linear sequence of facts and details, which included negations. "Arthur Danto at the age of forty had two daughters but no cat; he had aged; he had gray hairs": a series of photographs might show that the last two of these statements were not synonymous (because the graying came first in time), although a sequence of words so arranged might imply that they were; but no single image or set of them could show that all four statements applied, since in any one of them the cat might be there but out of sight, a third daughter hiding behind him, or his appearance temporarily youthful.[23] In other words, visual images may indeed make their affirmation in parallel to descriptive statements, but they will do so differently, by virtue of juxtaposition and integration, to produce what may be called a more "generic" kind of truth.

As Saint Augustine's remarks at the head of this chapter may be taken to suggest, truth of such a kind is not, or need not be, dependent on what is considered true in the way of a literal representation (as distinct from a literal image): one that shows forth what *is*, however that might be understood.[24] Rather, truth in this more generic sense of the word may be something that is assessed—actively, if one is alert; continuously, if one has the temperament—in terms of its relation to one's beliefs and its effect upon them.

To enlarge on the examples of the book jacket and the pair of hearts accordingly, there are three basic ways in which a visual image may be accounted true that are not subject, as the Courbet example is, to the relativity of the viewer's perceptions, or convertible into comparative terms of assessment without alteration in the process of the claim itself. First, the image may be true by virtue of its embodying a certain quality or effect: weightlessness, in the Toulouse-Lautrec lithograph, or what it is like to be without one's arms, as in a photograph of a nameless veteran of the Civil War (fig. 5). There is an equivalent to this in ordinary discourse in the way in which one speaks of a person as, say, a "true-blooded Irishman," meaning that he is the embodiment of certain Irish qualities, the possession of which is not really comparative with other outstandingly Irish persons, inasmuch as each of them would have a

5. An unidentified Union Civil War soldier, carte de visite photograph. Private collection.

different set of such qualities. It might similarly be thought that the defiance of gravity presented in the image of Loie Fuller was a relative feature of her dancing, such that images of Nureyev doing a grand jeté or of a champion high jumper would put what was shown here into place as an effect to which audiences responded. So indeed it might be, but it could also be the case that lightness and an airborne quality were particularly prized in dancers at the end of the nineteenth century, to the point of being deliberately cultivated, and that one sensed the application of this in Loie Fuller's case.

Second, the image may be taken as evidentially securing that something "was" or took place "out there," as when the imprint of a physical disturbance of some kind on a photographic negative is taken as testimony that there was some mysterious and rationally unexplainable intervention in the space that is being surveyed. Analogously, when the glazes in a

painting of Titian's become muddied with dirt and varnish, or
the tube top embedded in the paintwork of a Jackson Pollock
falls out, the work may need to be restored in order to be true to
the creative process; it no longer evidences what the artist did
on that surface, and it might be said that its "true surface"
needs to be put back or reconstituted. An equivalent here in
ordinary speech would lie in talking of the "true culprit" as
having been apprehended: one whose responsibility has been
secured on the basis of seemingly unimpeachable evidence or
authority. Indeed, in the classic detective story the process of
linking the evidence to the "true culprit" in this way, as
opposed to the false suspects, so that false clues are discarded
and true ones assembled by the end, is what gives the plot its
internal momentum.[25]

Last, a visual image may be accounted true in the Hegelian
sense that it shows forth certain social or political norms and
values that "belong" in a special sense to its historical time: as
Manet's *Execution of Maximilian* (fig. 6) may be taken as
summing up and summoning up visually how that event
seemed, to a Frenchman responding to the news of the emperor's death in distant Mexico and to what he heard and read
about it; or as Imogen Cunningham's photographs, taken in
the northwest mountains of Oregon in 1915, of a nude male
figure on a sheet of ice, encapsulate how it was possible then, as
it certainly would not be today, to "chase a naked husband
around Mount Rainier."[26] Manet's painting is by no means
literally true as a representation of what took place, since it is
based on eyewitness reports as printed in European news-
papers and on portrait photographs available or prints recon-
structing the scene, but it is truthful to how it all seemed (to
Manet as a Frenchman, learning about it in those ways) in such
details as the emperor's holding hands with his generals, his
standing upright as the volley was fired, the halolike hat on his
head.[27] Indeed, in comparing the changes made in the two later
versions it can be said Manet was balancing a sense of the
impersonal forces at work (as implied in the poses and faces of
the firing squad and the French uniforms that he showed them

22

6. Edouard Manet, *The Execution of Maximilian*, third version, 1867–68. Kunsthalle, Mannheim.

wearing) against whatever feelings of sympathy Maximilian's fate aroused in France, through the circumstances of his death and the way in which he met it.

A familiar verbal equivalent, then, to this "intervention" of the image back into history is to be found in the ascription of historical responsibility for an event to depersonalized forces of some kind, as in the orthodox Marxist's way of pointing to evidence of struggle between the classes.[28] And if one asks what is true in this Hegelian or Marxist sense, one must be prepared, unlike Pilate, to stay very long for an answer: the Manet did not begin to be thought of in the way described for almost a century. As against the claims of skepticism, it is in the nature of explanatory codes and how they allow us to deal with the world that the possibility of any determinative understanding or interpretation must itself be contextualized within social and intellectual history.[29] Now there are two perhaps radically opposed ways in which this claim, in respect to Manet's image, may be presented. Today, it may be said, we are able to see his images more completely than his contemporaries could: because we are at some distance (historically speaking) from his world, we can spell out conflicts or contradictions in his work which were then merely implicit. Alternatively, if the goal we set ourselves is to place the work in its original context—and that is one definition of the art historian's task—then such an account will seem misleading and ahistorical, which is, or corresponds to, the basic contention of the relativist.[30] But rather than entering further into the kind of theorizing that attaches to a Marxist or structuralist view of history, we may turn instead for an analogy to the nonrelativist claims of truth in the above cases, to the art of theater.

Proust remarked on what he called the "transparency" of the classical actress Berma,[31] and George Bernard Shaw, more analytic and questioning than Proust in his writings as a theater critic, illuminates in his discussion of Sarah Bernhardt what Proust was referring to here. He does this first by describing the kind of physical appearance that Bernhardt embodied: one conforming so markedly to contemporary ideals of beauty that its appeal could be given credence only in terms of those ideals: "Her lips are like a newly painted pillar box; her cheeks, right up to the languid lashes, have the bloom and surface of a peach; she is beautiful with the beauty of her school, and entirely inhuman and incredible." But this incredibility was "pardonable" because it was "so artful, so clever." Shaw then goes on to define—still in primarily visual or preverbal terms—how, in a typical first entrance, Bernhardt would use the occasion to secure before her viewers that she was in fact the person they took her for: "One feels, when the heroine bursts on the scene . . . that instead of imposing on you, she adds to her own piquancy by looking you straight in the face and saying, in effect: 'Now who would ever suppose that I am a grand-

mother?'" He interpreted this as a way of relaxing the claims
of credibility that she would otherwise make on her audience,
as she went on to more "serious business."

Shaw considered Bernhardt inferior to Eleonora Duse in
terms of all of those particular skills and the combination of
them that make great acting an art. But rather than comparing
the two, in terms of convincingness in the impression they gave,
what he did was to analyse (in another review) the very different ways in which Duse built up a "natural" effect. Duse
certainly created, in his perception, a more continuous and
integral kind of illusion. But since he could not help responding
to those qualities of immediacy and integrity that gave what
Bernhardt did its own kind of complete convincingness, he
ended his piece on her: "It is always Sarah Bernhardt in her
own capacity who does this to you. The dress, the title of the
play, the order of the words may vary; but the woman is always
the same. She does not enter into the leading character: she
substitutes herself for it."[32]

What contemporaries responded to in Bernhardt—what
they found true in the "transparent" sense of there not being
any other kind of truth to plumb beyond the immediate and
personal one—was peculiarly part of her historical identity as
an actress: an identity such that, in any other period or medium
of reception (as on film), what she did would not be measured
as great acting or successful illusion. It would appear absurd;
and when the "true" and the "absurd" present themselves in
counterpoint in this way, there can be no sliding scale between
them.

Narrative paintings are like theatrical performances in that
while they traditionally show characters and incidents deriving
from fiction, or represent reworkings of events from history,
they also contain elements or features that impress as being
true. Manet's *Execution* (fig. 6) aligns itself from this point of
view with the kind of performance that is "transparent."[33] It
was already criticized in its time for its appearance of emo-
tional disengagement from its subject, and the view earlier in
this century of what Manet did here was that he simply used the

materials at his disposal as a point of departure or pretext for pure paintwork for its own sake: which represents an equivalent in the case of picture making to the charge of absurdity in the case of acting. To those who take such a view, Goya's *The Third of May, 1808* (which Manet drew on for his first version) must seem like a paradigm of the bringing of direct experience to bear in a subject of this kind, to create a sense of authenticity that gives the work, emotionally rather than intellectually (or on a strictly factual basis) the stamp and redolence of truth.[34] But the Manet in fact belongs to another class of visual image: one that does not need to impress by virtue of its match to an existing story, or to rest its effect of believability on the fitting together of accumulated and sequentially integrated details, as in the Dusean version of acting.

Caravaggio's late painting of the burial of Saint Lucy (fig. 7), done for the church of that saint in Syracuse, is like the Manet in that the truth that can be read into it as a narrative image rests on a different basis than conformity to the details of an existing and known story. It shows a historical occurrence in the sense of making its nature visually accessible; but though the martyrdom itself was familiar, it or its aftermath had rarely been depicted in previous art, and the representation really needed its title in order to give a clear identity to its components.[35] The grave and tragic quality that is imparted by the color, grouping, and the expressions and the huge void of space around and above the figures establish together a mood for the presentation: one embracing both the death and the tenor of response to it. The arched and shadowed opening at the back left may represent the entrance to the catacombs of Syracuse, but if so this is inessential, since, from a narrative standpoint, the setting is quite minimal and even empty in the contribution that it makes. Nor are there references incorporated to traditional religious subject matter or to the typology of existing images that deal with death and suffering, as there are in the Goya, to render the choice of imagery more telling.[36] Rather, actions and movements are used to suggest the intrusion of the contingent into the rite of mourning and burial that is being

26

7. Michelangelo da Caravaggio, *The Martyrdom of Saint Lucy*, 1608.
Church of Santa Lucia, Syracuse.

performed; especially in the looming foreground figures of the gravediggers.

In the Manet, in an era when photographic images of public occasions and incidents were being increasingly looked to for their revelation of comparable qualities of "contingency,"[37] there is an analogous inclusion of elements—such as the group of bystanders watching form behind the wall and the white cemetery chapel at the back left—that are justified in principle by the received details of a "story" report, but have no concrete basis there for their specification in this fashion. But the connective relationships of such elements to the presentation as a whole are (or at least, to those uninitiated into Manet's procedures here, appear to be) structurally more illogical. The underlying distinction to which one is led is that, while Caravaggio's viewers believed firmly in the saintliness of Saint Lucy and looked on the circumstances of her death and burial as accepted fact, for Manet's potential viewers questions of truth and belief regarding what had happened to Maximilian were more overlaid with uncertainty, and yet at the same time (insofar as they could be formulated in a case like this) more open to empirical scrutiny.[38]

There are, in sum, images of a story-telling kind that represent events that actually did occur (though they may require reconstitution from the limited data or factual records available). There are also ones that conjure up imaginatively events as they might have occurred (even though it may seem most improbable or quite impossible that they actually occurred at all). In any particular period, whether a narrative subject is placed under the first or second of these headings may be a matter of choice or of intrinsic belief. Saint Luke painting the Virgin, for instance, is a common subject in Renaissance art, based upon an early legend, and no doubt it seemed to skeptics —even before it was interpreted by painters as a visionary subject—that it was improbable that a man, who already appeared quite old at the time he visited the Virgin and painted the Christ child, should have lived at least another thirty-three years to write his Gospel after that. By contrast, a modern image of the capture and arrest of Hitler in the jungles of the Amazon represents a subject that, even for those who might like to think that it occurred, is intrinsically suspect in its authenticity. Both kinds of image can nevertheless, as in the workings of stage performance—which provides analogies in both cases—impress as having a quality of truth to them. In the first case it will rest (as on record covers) on the convincingness of the details, as they are put together or "bracketed" with one another; in the second it will rest (as in advertising images) on the kinds of persuasiveness that attach to the character of the medium itself.

# Chapter Two

# Painting and Advertising: The Force
# of Implication and Suggestion

*In all of the pictures in which Raphael has represented the apostles, he
has drawn them with great nobleness; he has given them as much
dignity as the human figure is capable of receiving; yet we are expressly
told in scripture they had no such respectable appearance; and of Saint
Paul in particular we are told by himself, that his* bodily *presence was*
mean.

SIR JOSHUA REYNOLDS, DISCOURSE 4

*When we speak of a work of art—above all of one by Rembrandt—we
speak not of an untruth, but of something imagined which is not its
contrary either. . . .*

EUGÈNE FROMENTIN[1]

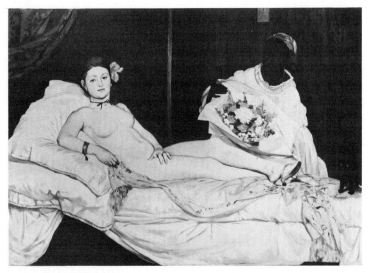

8.  Edouard Manet, *Olympia*, 1863. Musée du Louvre, Paris.

THERE IS A CONCERN in the history of philosophy, going all the way back to Plato, about the capacity of paintings and other visual images and artifacts to instill false, or to encourage putatively true, beliefs. How does this idea of the way visual images work—by power of implication and suggestion inherent in the nature of the image—apply to a modern painting which is imaginatively charged for the viewer both in its subject and in the presentation of that subject?

We can take for this purpose Manet's *Olympia*[2] (fig. 8). It is frequently compared with the contemporary nudes of Gérôme (fig. 9) to bring out its character, and the point of these comparisons is to suggest, in shorthand, how Manet's nude is the truer because Gérôme's represents a stereotype of womanhood: one that superimposes a traditional, male-dominated set of values onto the presentation of female appearance and behavior. Now just because the presentation is so readily recognizable from this point of view, someone could always find the Gérôme nude to be truer—in the same sense as they could find a Breton truer than a Courbet. One may, that is, just choose to like what one likes, in ignorance of, or in deliberate opposition to, the dictates of modern tastes. One may like pictures in which the impedimenta or the body parts have a worked up, shiny kind of finish, and also ones that do not "jump out" of the frame at you. One may say, "That's true (real) painting." So what can a claim about truth in the *Olympia* assert, other than the difference between the two works?

The *Olympia* is not true in a representational sense (by virtue of likeness) since it involves both a favorite model close to the artist posing in the nude for him *and* the representation of a fictional character. It shows, in the same sort of way as Rembrandt's Saskia-as-Flora, an actual person playing an assigned role; and it is also like the same artist's Hendrickje Stoffels-as-Bathsheba in the use of a model as the centerpiece of a fictional narrative.[3] What Manet does here is to combine those two

9. Jean Léon Gérôme, *The Slave Market,* c. 1870. Sterling and
Francine Clark Art Institute, Williamstown, Massachusetts.

processes of imaginative construction, which are normally somewhat distinct in the way they are apprehended, and the effect of this is to transform as well as embellish the self-presentation of the person he used. That a high-class courtesan known to him may have looked like this, or that such courtesans in general acted in this sort of way, simply adds an additional factor, that of plausibility.[4] And how exactly plausibility of appearance differs from truth in this connection is brought out by the example of matching actress to part: it depends not on any necessity of resemblance, but on there being a sufficient number of corresponding features, within a very broad range.

Nor is the *Olympia* true in a depictional sense (by virtue of cogency and coherence), since its detail and specificity are essentially of a "playing card" kind. The other later nineteenth-century artist of whom this is true is Cézanne, and if one considers that Cézanne made all the women that he painted look like tanks, then it does not matter how much concentrated attention he gave to specific details and features in any one of his paintings of Mme. Cézanne: she still comes out looking tanklike, this being a matter of *emphasis* on the artist's part, at the expense of a coherent physical shapeliness.

Nor finally is the *Olympia* true in a referential (convention-governed) sense, since the relevant "codes" for reading such an image available to a contemporary viewer are either confused or broken with. Expectations of such a subject are in fact defeated by Manet's form of presentation in two different ways; or one might say they are *inverted*, since the violence of responses to the work when it was publicly shown implies not blockage, but rather misdirection. First, the adoption of a pose and setting directly recalling Titian's famous *Venus of Urbino* in the Uffizi carried a special pointedness in terms of how Manet used it here, in drawing on the understanding of the time that Titian's reclining figure was to be taken as being a prostitute. Contemporary viewers had no problem in responding to Cabanel's *Birth of Venus* (fig. 10), which was the outstanding public success of the Salon in 1863, two years before the *Olympia* appeared there, as an indulgent fantasy image of relaxed female sexuality exposed to view—one representing, with its breaking wavelets and attendant putti, a prurient version of Raphael's *Galatea* subject, and one given viability by that association. But Manet's associative reference, on the other hand, to a well-known masterpiece of past art and its application to Olympia's own form of queenliness, in the way in which she put her physical charms on display, was in fact lost, except on one or two critics.

This in turn leads on to the subject, which, in the basic connotations of pose and setting together, is of a type that had currency in erotic prints of the time, and in photographs (fig. 11) that comparably used an available model.[5] Details of the setting, such as Manet also includes—drapes, a bed cover—are used there to show off the nudity; the recumbent figure, like his, looks outward as she lies there. Such images were created, or at least put into circulation, for the private use and pleasure of an exclusively male audience. Their syntactical readability depends essentially on the implication of a spatial continuity between the viewer's own position in relation to the image and the part of the room where the figure herself lies; and with this there goes the sense of a receptivity to the viewer's presence in the character of the gaze. The viewer is put into the position of a male visitor entering the contained space that the nude occupies or standing on its threshold, pausing in expectation of how he will be received there, before moving up to the bed for a promised encounter in which she will be properly submissive to the claims of his masculine self-assertiveness. Voyeurism thereby becomes a substitute for the sexual encounter itself. Manet, in contrast, defeats that kind of readability through the way in which he shows the drape and falling bedclothes, set completely parallel to the picture's surface and virtually identified with it, so that continuity with the viewer's space is denied; and through the directly open and, therefore, challenging quality which he gives to Olympia's gaze.

The *Olympia* has nevertheless *become* true—for us today—in the explicitness of the sexuality that it offers: as in the position of hand on the thigh, which draws attention to the

10. Alexandre Cabanel, *The Birth of Venus,* 1863. Musée du Louvre, Paris.

11. F. J. Moulin, Nude, photograph, c. 1860. Bibliothèque
Nationale, Paris.

pubic area rather than concealing it, and the motifs of the black
ribbon around the neck and the footwear still on, which serve
to offset the nudity. It has become true in the directly visible
evidence that its markings in paint present of Manet's attitude
to process, so that the declaration of "paint as paint" on its
surface comes to register as a form of sincerity. And above all it
has become true for the way in which it evokes Manet's challenge to the academic situation of his time: its standards and its
constraints. It could be said, in fact, that the form of "truth"
which it represents in these three different ways was understood only too well at its original showing, in the sense of being
angrily and peremptorily rejected. All of this we acknowledge
and explain, in offering up the comparison of Manet and
Gérôme. And if the effectiveness of the challenge that the
Olympia posed is now debated afresh, or reinterpreted in the
light of what is accounted "true" and why, it will be in social
and political terms.[6] Some women, it may be said, are in social

and sexual conformity with the type of femininity that Gérôme puts on display, which could be an issue of class. Or it may be argued that the projection of a sexuality that is direct in addressing the viewer, rather than conducive to male fantasies of self-gratification, is in conflict with the more personal associations and references that Manet's imagery incorporates. The issue is then one of "public" and "private" meanings and of their incomplete intersection or congruence in a case of this sort.

Now one could call what is being appealed to in all of this a "metaphorical" as opposed to a "literal" kind of truth, in one (very loose) usage of the word *metaphor*, because it has to do with the interaction of the *Olympia* with other figurative elements within the composition—the maid with the flowers, the bristling cat—and the implications that this carries for us as viewers respondent to her pose and gaze.[7] If one did so, it would be with the understanding that metaphors *can* in principle serve to make assertions, and to express a "real truth" about the world; they are not simply fanciful departures from a more normal or standard descriptive vocabulary.[8] It would also be with the understanding that neither the Gérôme nude nor the erotic photograph (figs. 9, 10) represent "literal" truth here. One may be said to entail literality of *representation* in its undisguised dependence for anatomy and physique on the use of a studio model; the other, literality of *depiction* in showing the soles of the feet dirty, as if indeed the model had just stepped over the studio floor to take her place on the bed. (The first would be comparable to the use of actual wine or a zipper in a theatrical performance, the second to a person actually falling or choking on stage and making this part of the act.) The differing properties of the two images that are in question here may then be accounted for according to the way in which such results are arrived at in their respective media: that is, according to a causal idea of truth, much favored as a basis for distinguishing between painting and photography. Photography has, however, in a case like this or in still life, its own kind of principles for keying together the differing elements of the "given"; and the fact that both these nude images bring up an implied attitude on the viewer's part—albeit more passive ones than in the case of the *Olympia*—makes them equally, for present purposes, fictions.

It would be more valid, therefore, to talk in all these cases of implications or of a suggestiveness, which the work takes on or comes to carry. It then becomes possible to compare the kinds of implication that are present in advertising images that have a female presence as their subject, and the ways in which they are put to work on the viewer. Take for instance the features of Catherine Deneuve (fig. 12) as they appear in an advertisement for Chanel No. 5. The corresponding implication here is that Deneuve's special beauty is of a kind that offers itself to the viewer in a potent, sexually charged form. This is a proposition that cannot be detached from the realm of fiction, except by an act of will or with special knowledge, since it is in the medium of film that the glamour of Deneuve is embodied artistically,

12. "Catherine Deneuve for Chanel," advertisement for Chanel No. 5, 1976. Courtesy of Artmedia Variétés, Paris.

secured through familiarity, and directorially codified. What turns the implication into an insinuation about the possibility of acquiring glamour in general is the suggestion, put over by the accompanying words conjoining name and product, that the use of the perfume itself confers what the viewer needs and desires here.[9] The feminist recognizes this as a false intimation, concerning availability, imposed onto the true sources of attractiveness in Deneuve; or it may come to be so recognized through protracted exposure. Another way of dealing with the intimation, less resistant to it or questioning of its truth, is to take it as a form of "play-acting" in which the subject has been cast—without prescriptive force addressed to one's physical and moral being, but simply so as to set the imagination working by conjuring up "worlds" of being other than the one in which we happen to be fixed. To think of the use of Chanel No. 5 in relation to Catherine Deneuve then becomes a desirable association for us, in the same sense as the idea of drinking Spanish sherry as one would in Spain is a desirable association on a cold winter's night in Pittsburgh. What is entailed here appears, in that light, as a special kind of "removed" truth— the converse of what will later be termed mendacity—which is pleasing just because it is so artfully done.

Alternatively one might compare, for the workings of suggestion, a very different kind of photographic image, taken in Occupied Paris during the Second World War (fig. 13). The particular image chosen, *Velo-Taxi*,[10] is one that implies the lack of gasoline then; the limitations of public transportation that emptied the streets and brought in this form of conveyance as an alternative for those who counted on getting somewhere; and the contrast between those who had money for such things and those who were put into the position of acting as coolie for them. It is an image that intimates, more generally, something about deprivation and the cunning and resourcefulness needed to survive under such circumstances. A German of the Occupation force might not have seen it as true in those ways, but he might come to do so with time.

We can then see more clearly, in this light, the progressive

40

13. Robert Cohen, *Velo-Taxi during the Occupation in Paris,*
photograph, 1940. Courtesy of Institut National de l'Audiovisuel,
Paris.

shift, or process of conversion, from image that can be taken
literally (just that alone) to "metaphor": as in Barthes's photograph of his mother as a young girl in the Winter Garden,
belonging amongst other images that he had of her at different
ages, which after her death became the one in which he could
find her complete identity condensed; [11] or as in the photograph by André Kertesz of a Red hussar leaving Budapest in
June 1919, excerpted from a larger episode of a departure to
show, according to John Berger, a moment of recognition
between the soldier and the woman carrying their child that
stands in opposition to the larger patterns of history. [12] We can
understand also how portraits of a highly artificial, grandiose
kind can become the embodiment of period manners and life
styles, as in later eighteenth-century England; how Poussin's
archaeological accuracy can become understood as an earnest
of truth, even in mythological subjects; and how the showing
of biblical figures in contemporary dress—in itself an accepted

*In 1902, while traveling on her first train journey to the West, Mrs. Mary Ann Kroll audaciously lit up a cigarette.*

*Her husband promptly set her on the right track.*

VIRGINIA SLIMS

You've come a long way, baby.

14. "You've come a long way, baby," advertisement for Virginia Slims Lights (upper half only). Courtesy of Philip Morris, U.S.A.

convention—can, like the concocted scenes of the past in the Virginia Slims cigarette advertisements (fig. 14), distill a period for us and its difference from our own.

Is it possible to put this shift or process of conversion into any kind of historical perspective, so that the steps in between, in the case of either language or visual images, are clarified in terms of successive phases that they represent and of differences from phase to phase in the way that the changes work themselves out? Since no single work of art or set of images from the past allows this without a great deal of background information and contextualization of its subject matter, it may be best to begin by constructing an example that entails the use of a set of words making up a simple sentence, with greater shifts over time than would normally be the case. It is an example that is essentially imaginary in its workings, but it is based in some of its aspects on historical fact.

Let us say, then, that after the failure of the Jacobite Rebellion in 1745–46, when defeat of his forces at Culloden has forced Bonnie Prince Charlie to make his escape from Scotland, the phrase "the prince has gone over the water" comes into use as a statement of fact. It denotes that a certain person called the "prince" or the "Young Pretender" has taken a boat to the Hebrides, and from there has gone by ship to France; and this event comes to be referred to in the phrase and thereby recognized. A person saying this as a statement of fact, which at the time might prove *not* to have been true, does not, it should be noted, commit himself to recognition of the subject as (in fact) prince. The term *prince* could be spoken sarcastically or put in quotes, to make clear that one did not consider *that* to be fact; and also there are two different passages that might be referred to.

At a second phase in the history of the phrase, members of a sect meet and evolve a ritual in which they use these words: let us suppose that they stand to attention and drink a toast saying this—thereby affirming their membership in the sect and formulating at the same time their assent to a belief system, which entails the wished-for restoration of the Stuart dynasty. To belong to the sect is to learn and participate in the use of a coded set of symbols and rituals (an iconography). And the version of truth that comes into operation here may be termed *existential*, in that the words used directly assert and acknowledge a commitment of belief to what is held to be true. Later, other people join the sect, no longer working for that Restoration—or even knowing, perhaps, to whom the words refer— but still affirming their membership by saying those words as they drink their port. The words are now detached from their earlier import and become a purely evocative element in the ritual. Finally, in the modern period there is a version of the sect where people still use the words to affirm their membership, but they use them in a nonserious (ironic and parodic) way: they dress up as Bonnie Prince Charlie and his friends (without knowing anything about what they were actually like or what they wore), parade around the room saying these words and toasting one another with them, and so on.[13]

There are of course analogies to those phases in the history of "signs." The signs of the Masonic Order include the schematic representation of various tools, such as the level and triangle, which (by the early nineteenth century) are grouped and organized in arrangements that diagram the rituals and ceremonies of the order. Somewhat later, the same basic images are used in popular prints that affirm the solidarity of the workers, in the manual and industrial arts.[14] Later still, in a painting of Vuillard's, one such image, the T-square or Tau, is shown in a more suggestive and even mysterious fashion, appearing on the wall above a figure lying in bed. Finally, the sculptor Carl André in 1969–70 lays two cut segments of wood one on top of the other to form the same basic configuration and calls the piece "Tau," for what are now purely associative reasons, which are also totally desacralized.

While it may not be possible to isolate a process like this from one painting or version of a subject to another, there are also cases where a shift or process of conversion such as those examples illustrate is to be found in the generation of a specific work, and how it is correspondingly read. In Carpaccio's *Young Knight in a Landscape* of 1510 (fig. 15) the inflectional shift from a portrait image—which could have been created independently and not necessarily for this purpose—to a conceptual representation is marked out in the discrepancy of scale between head and hands and the superimposition of the figure as a single structural unit onto a landscape rich in natural and material details, so that while in a posture of alertness, the knight seems distanced from the intense activity taking place there.[15] While these are intriguing elements of the work's constructive make-up, it is not so much the structure itself that reveals why a young man should be posing in this way, as it is certain iconographic details and their positioning that make this into an allegory of vigilant Christian knighthood. A viewer of the time, even observing or knowing that it was built around a portrayal, would be dependent on those details, including the motto on the tree and the ermine, for the understanding of why

15. Vittore Carpaccio, *Young Knight in a Landscape*, 1510(?).
Thyssen-Bornemisza Collection, Lugano.

16. Rembrandt van Ryn, *Self-Portrait*, c. 1660. The Iveagh Bequest, Kenwood. Courtesy of The Greater London Council as Trustees.

a particular young man—now identified on the basis of those elements as Francesco Maria della Rovere, the young duke of Urbino—was so depicted. Iconographic interpretation, in other words, serves as an exegetic extension here of the way in which the different elements are positionally encoded: it ratifies and gives a discursive shape to what can be intuited from the organization of those elements in relation to one another. The same also holds true in principle for Rembrandt's late *Self-*

17. Gustave Courbet, *The Sculptor*, 1844. Present whereabouts
unknown.

*Portrait* (fig. 16) which has parts of two large circles inscribed
on the background wall. Those circles may derive from a
certain kind of wall map that hung on the walls of Dutch
houses, which have been simplified and abstracted to appear as
they do for structural reasons; but it is highly unlikely that they
exist here *only* for this reason, and so the basic sense in which
they are recognized as a "metaphor," in the stress on the
quality of geometric ordering that they impose, leads in turn to
such putative suggestions as that they may refer to the per-
fection of God, or be emblems of theory and practice in art.[16]

In a mid-nineteenth-century version of the theme of artistic
creation by Courbet (fig. 17), set outdoors amid rocks and
trees, water issues from a circular orifice to the right, adjacent
to the posing figure's protruding knee and his groin; and immediately above it there appears the figure of a woman on her
back, which is to be taken as having been carved out of the
rock. The title *The Sculptor* and the use of Courbet's own facial
features supply the additional idea here that it is the artist
himself who has brought this figure into being, and that his
narcissistic pose in nature is related to his having done this.[17]
The woman may also represent the genius loci, but those
implications are supplemental rather than necessary to the
basic metaphor itself, which is clear in its own right, from the
relationship of the elements described, as being sexual in
nature. Here then, more specifically and absolutely than in the
Rembrandt, the underlying *condensation* of associations that
makes for an effect of metaphor is embodied in the character of
the imagery itself.

Nor do the elements that accomplish such an effect necessarily have to be of a figurative kind. Robert Rauschenberg's
*Factum I* and *Factum II* of 1957 (fig. 18) consist of two images,
made up of photographic fragments and cuttings pasted on and
paintwork over and around them, the second of which repeats
the first almost exactly, but with some minor differences. Here,
the way in which the second image does differ from the first,
insofar as it cannot be accidental or purely casual in nature,
becomes singled out—by *excerption* from the imagery as a
whole—as a matter of attention in its own right.[18] Also the
processes entailed in the making of a copy are recalled to the
viewer and evoked, as being part of the act that brought this
piece of "duplication" into being. The difference in this example, then, is that now the recognition of the "metaphor" is
entirely and, one might say, axiomatically dependent on structural and technical considerations.

Also to be considered is the case of portraiture. By the second
half of the fourteenth century already, Italian art encompassed
images of the great and famous that were designed to be taken

18. Robert Rauschenberg, *Factum I* and *Factum II,* 1957. Panza
Collection, Milan; collection of Morton G. Neumann, Chicago.

literally—as is indicated by corresponding stories about their
creation, and by the conventions of praise adopted:[19] not, it
should be noted, for the furnishing of a literal image (as defined
in chap. one) but for the literal *representation* entailed, which
might include the accoutrements of office, or the action of a
hand that does something specific and concrete. Portrait
images could also be put into a context that included other
persons or objects bearing on the known personality of the
man or woman in question, and the elements used for this
purpose were like the attributes of saints, in being associated
with the person in a way that indemnified his or her identity.
For a saint such as Lucy or Catherine, that is, the inclusion of
the eyes and the wheel avoided confusion with other saints, and

at the same time evoked and impressed on the memory the form of her martyrdom; and the showing of a collector with objects that he owned correspondingly incorporated the act of collecting into history, rather than allowing it to be lost with time. Alternatively, a "play-acting" kind of situation could be devised for the portrayal: one that expanded upon traits of character and behavior that were associated with the person and that were taken as practically or ideally manifest in the life that he or she lived. Such presentations needed to be like the representations of saints in *sacra conversazione* form: appropriate, in the sense that they fitted with what was known or taken for granted about the person's character and way of life, as when donors are shown kneeling in the wings or landscape of an altarpiece; and believable, in accordance with a certain view of the workings of the world and the interworkings of the natural and the divine, as when Chancellor Rolin is shown by van Eyck with the Madonna and Child before him. In all three of those cases working from the model as a "given" could be a point of departure for the artist; however, the processes of working to which that source material was submitted would vary, as would the imaginative uses made of it.

It is clear from Reynold's fourth discourse that the triple division of portrait images on those lines continued down to the eighteenth century into the age of "heroic" portraiture (full-scale and historical) and the "grand style," with the only distinction being that the genres of portrayal became more strictly and hierarchically categorized, with a "more permanent" form of dress or with one that evoked an earlier period in a desirable and accessible way, placed above "temporary fashion"; both forms of portrayal were rated above the kind that concentrated upon "minute breaks and peculiarities in the face," rather than "approaching [the subject] to a general idea."[20] It is misleading to make a dichotomy of portraits into those that are purely or primarily descriptive and those that carry moral, intellectual, social, and political implications, on the grounds of there being a supporting iconography that is used on one side and not on the other, insofar as there are many intermediate or combinational kinds of portrait, in which an image that would otherwise (or at an earlier point in its generation) ask to be taken literally takes on the force of a "metaphor"—much as the profile portraits do on Renaissance coins and medals.

Does the coming of photography (in the 1830s) make a difference here? It does not in terms of the inclusion of attributes or of "play-acting"—since both of those are given a place in portrait photography from the beginning and continue to have a place in certain cases (such as book or record jackets). But it does make a difference in terms of how seriously the quality of "metaphor" is taken. For it is in the nature of photography as a medium—the conditions of generation and reproduction that set it apart from other visual media—that it sets new standards for what it means for an image to be taken literally, and that it does so even alongside painting and in competition with it (as is still true today). This is why, in its bringing together and specific physical focusing of anatomical and natural elements, Courbet's *Sculptor* (fig. 17) is likely to appear affected—and by that token untruthful, even as a powerfully evocative "metaphor"—in the way that the Rembrandt, as a self-portrait also, does not. It may be true to his character, but it does not "look" true.

Here a return to the opening point in this chapter, the capacity of images to instill false beliefs, seems relevant. Paintings and photographs, it might be argued, really need different treatment here, for while all paintings are in a sense fabrications (depictions of some subject as seen or interpreted by the artist), photographs are in one respect always true to life. The painter forms, while the photographer frames an image. Consequently, when photographs are untrue it can be because they have been consciously doctored, as when fan magazines fabricate images falsely implying that two movie stars are entering the same hotel room. A Quattrocento painter showing the Holy Family and donors in one visual space is not, by contrast, offering us an image of that sort. Nobody in the fifteenth century would have thought such an altarpiece to imply that the donors were thus acquainted with the Holy Family. To suppose that the juxta-position in such cases represents anything other than the con-struction of an ideal or suppositional kind of relationship, expressed in similelike form, is to import an essentially modern conception of visual truth into a quite inappropriate earlier context. It would, however, be a mistake to imply that such worries about pictorial truth are just worries regarding the truth of photographs, for these kinds of concern which pho-tographic examples raise can be found in painting even prior to the invention of photography. This can best be brought out by considering the "play" with truth that takes place in certain modern paintings which are more complex in imagery, as a text may also be, and the terms on which it justifies itself there.

In 1790 David was invited by the Jacobin Society to execute a painting, to hang in the National Assembly, of the oath taken in the Jeu de Paume at Versailles in June of the previous year, when the representatives of the Third Estate who gathered there made a solemn pledge of their commitment and common purpose (fig. 19). It was to be both a record of the occasion and a commemoration of its significance; motivated by what he would later call a "[devouring] love of liberty," David planned the undertaking on an enormous scale. He would report in his notes, having probably been a witness himself, on what had taken place; at the same time he would draw on written and verbal accounts to project an appropriate range of emotions, amongst those shown taking part. As the mass of deputies crowding in receded further back into complete anonymity, enthusiasm and support were to be suggested by convergences of movement; toward the edges, more independently consti-tuted patterns of gesture and expression would imply that affirmation was merging into acclaim; and in the foreground, the protagonists of the oath itself, portrayed wherever possible from the life, would appear in a heroic central grouping and in solemn poses of recognition to either side. The circumstances of the Revolution, however, and David's own participation in

52

19. Jacques-Louis David, *The Oath of the Tennis Court*, drawing, 1790. Musée de Versailles.

it, prevented him from ever progressing beyond a few preliminary sketches and studies. Consequently in 1798 he
reached the point of having to petition the Members of the
Directory for financial support in order to start afresh. Empha-
sizing the sheer magnitude of the project, he added in a post-
script that, now that he no longer had available to him those
who had made up the legislative body of that time and "who
are mostly, between ourselves, quite insignificant for poster-
ity," his intention was "to substitute all those who have
become illustrious since and are for this reason much more
interesting. . . ." It was true, he wrote, that it would be an
anachronism to do this, but it would be one that famous
painters had resorted to before, and one for which people
would be grateful. Given that (as he put it earlier in the petition) things were calmer, sanity received more recognition, and
people's feelings were more settled, such a plan of substitution
commended itself not just as a practical expedient, but for the
contribution that it would make—as a matter of economy, one
might say, with effect here substituting for cause—to a
stronger embodiment of what was now perceived as the ethos
of the event.[21]

Goya's portrait of the duchess of Alba, dated 1797 and
inscribed "Solo Goya" (fig. 20), shows her standing in a landscape setting of river and trees and pointing with her right hand
on which she wears two rings, one inscribed "Goya" and the
other "Alba," at the signature in the ground at her feet. This
emblematic conjunction has often been taken as a pledge of
fidelity to his loved one on Goya's part and her acknowl-
edgment of it. Certainly if one compares the portrait that Goya
had done of her in a landscape of soft blues and greens a year or
two earlier—when their intimacy was developing toward its
apogee, in a stay that they enjoyed together after her husband's
death on her country estate—there is no very marked difference in the way that Goya presents her appearance and behavior. Around 1797, however, he would add to his series of
prints the *Caprices* that were then in progress, a plate that he
later suppressed: titled "The Dream of Lies and Inconstancy,"

20. Francisco de Goya y Lucientes, *The Duchess of Alba,* 1797.
Courtesy of the Hispanic Society of America, New York.

it shows the duchess as a two-faced beauty with strange
diaphanous wings, who fondles Goya with one hand while her
other arm is extended toward a rival lover and an accomplice
or servant places her hand in his. Rather than being an affirmation of her beauty and her attachment to the artist alone, the
portrait may be seen in this light as an ironic affirmation of
what the lady cannot, of her very nature, be. *Solo Goya*, cut in
the rock as indicated by the shadowing of the letters (not
inscribed in sand as lovers traditionally *also* did with their
names), would then be a signature that functions to secure, in
autographic form of testimony within the painting, the validity
of the underlying perception.[22] It would imply Goya's ability—
and his alone as an artist—to see through the duchess's beauty
and her fashionableness, so richly on display here. The landscape setting with its distinct areas of coloring that evoke all
four elements—earth and fire as well as water and air—and its
sexually charged shapes would suggest how she is in fact
changeable, like the river in its course, and fickle, like the misty
overhanging atmosphere. The larger intimation of the images
brought together into this portrayal, with its structure that
effects a condensation of different and even contrary principles, is then that love may alter—it automatically does so,
like the elements themselves—but art, *Goya's* art, as an instrument of detached observation recording what lies beyond or
behind appearance, endures.

Seurat, in his *Sunday Afternoon at the Grande Jatte* of
1884–86 (fig. 21), chose for subject the island on the Seine that
had been newly adopted by the middle classes of Paris as an
agreeable place to visit, within ready access from the city, and
as a setting for their weekend leisure activities. The presence of
stoves provided as an amenity for cooking waffles (the little
girls to the right sit beside one), the hooped crinoline skirt that
had just come into high fashion at the time, the habit that was
in vogue then of walking a pet monkey on a leash; these are
factual aspects of what Seurat shows as taking place on the
island. But there are equally touches of playful humor throughout: the receding stretch of island with its grass and trees is

21. Georges Seurat, *Sunday Afternoon on the Island of La Grande Jatte*, 1884–86. Collection of The Art Institute of Chicago.

presented in a panoramic view, so that every available pocket of space is seen as filled up with contrasting kinds of pursuit; the extreme tip of the umbrella of a disappearing woman is to be recognized, along with the tip of her skirt; and figures and props are organized throughout so that, in the two-dimensional scheme of the design, they touch one another at one point and one point only. Hieratic frozen poses are used to imply, by fairly explicit association, a ritual quality to the proceedings of the kind found in Egyptian or Assyrian art or in the frescoes of Piero della Francesca. And Seurat's deeper perception about the use of the island comes out in the way in which facial expressions and patterns of behavior that are totally isolated from one another in psychological terms intimate what it meant to such people—shown here as types rather than individuals—to participate in separate ways, yet in immediate proximity to others, in this collectively shared context of relaxation and enjoyment.[23] The painting thus becomes like a set of extended metaphors, giving concrete embodiment to what happens when a time and setting invite congregation of this sort, and yet at the same time going beyond proverbial wisdom on the subject, in endowing each of the participants with his or her own distinct form of response to the occasion.

All three of the possibilities for a "play with truth" described in those paintings are to be found together in a recent example of fashion advertising (Leslie Fay, "Whenever It's Time for a Dress" [1981]). The men and women shown together in this photographic creation in rich, very prominent colors and textures are such as could not reasonably be expected to belong, in terms of overall physical appearance, to a single family or social set. They have been chosen and brought together precisely for the sake of a larger kind of representativeness, which involves economy. The furnishings of the room—a grand

22. *Sunday Afternoon on the Island of La Grande Jatte,* detail.

piano with a flower arrangement on it, decorative china on inset shelves, an early American portrait, a gold mantel clock, the rug, and so on—are there to suggest a common taste, to set against the variety of the dresses. It extends by implication to the silver, glass, and china that are being used, and, by a condensation of suggestion, to the food and drink that are being consumed. Within the space of what is evidently a very large room, forms of grouping and interchange project a shared consciousness amongst these people of enjoying themselves in one another's company, as proverbial wisdom supposes to be the case, yet each in his or her fashion. Since the medium is photography here, the total effect of all this comes out as somewhat absurd: poses are being maintained as if in complete detachment from any physical actuality, and the fingers resting on the man's shoulder at the top right appear as if they might belong to the man in the portrait. But the larger intimation is perfectly clear: that is, the truth that there is a definite relationship between patterns of social behavior and the kind of clothes that one wears—as well as with the furnishings of the settings in which one congregates and the particular people with whom one associates—is overlaid with a falsehood, that wearing such dresses will make one privy to "wonderful moments in life" (as the running text below calls them) of the kind depicted here.

Here, and subsequently in our "readings" of advertising images, we are attributing complex and rather clearly defined intentions to the producers of those images. And doing that seems an appropriate procedure. The advertiser aims for his message to come across without ambivalence, he desires that the visual rhetoric of the image be unmistakable; even if we are not clear why his image succeeds in that regard, we do know its desired or intended effect. We can appropriately speak of such images, then, in terms of the truth or falsity of the beliefs that they are intended to produce in the viewer. We read such images with confidence just because they are intended for us. But in looking at images from earlier times it may be less clear whether we can so readily interpret them. What is available to

us now may at best be an archeological reconstruction of the
truth of these images.

Hence we may naturally ask how far can this kind of a "play
with truth" in visual images be pushed back in time? Though
what happens earlier may be more dependent on iconographic
"coding" and the transformations that lead away from the
"given" in experience may be less structurally marked, the
intermix of record and fancy, of the observed and the imagined
that occurs in any particular case will not in itself be to the
point. Rather, the general principle deriving from the preceding examples to govern the application of the term will be that a
"play with truth" occurs when what is shown conflicts directly
with the capacity of the image to be taken literally.

In the theory of the visual arts, in antiquity and again from
the early Renaissance down to the modern period, discussion
of the possibilities of beguilement and dupery that painting
presents stays within a framework established by ancient and
medieval philosophizing on the subject. It is limited, both
theoretically and interpretatively, to the potential that painting
has for conveying the physical presence of three- dimensional
images on a two-dimensional surface, and to the way in which
the creative imagination (Ital.: *fantasia*) can conjure up visually
what does not actually exist but might exist, such as giants or
monsters.[24] There is, however, also the term *conceit* (Ital.:
*concetto*), which has become a familiar one for art as well as
literature by the later sixteenth century. It signifies, in both
cases equally, a device of presentation or illusion of a fanciful,
self-consciously inventive kind. It is a term that can be used
correspondingly both for associative devices, such as Caravaggio's clothing of the young men in his *Calling of Matthew* in
Venetian costume of a century earlier,[25] and also for deliberate
stylistic archaisms, such as the creation in the early sixteenth
century by Pontormo and others of portraits that hark back to
a mode of presentation that was current in the Quattrocento.[26]
In both of these cases the mode of presentation is one that
qualifies mere visual semblance in the subjects with the aura
that it attaches to them of an earlier time and place. The best

term, accordingly, for what takes place here may be *mendacity*, denoting a deliberated kind of invention that makes in such cases for an effect of artificial suspension between the present and the past. Such conceits do not necessarily appear only in a secular context, or one of courtly patronage, but the spirit of presumptive license which *mendacity* implies is most apparent in its workings there: as in the mendacious historicism of both incident and presentation that characterizes Taddeo Zuccaro's decorations for the Farnese family at Caprarola (1565);[27] or in a more familiar example from the seventeenth century, the flattering manipulation of historical occasions in Rubens's Marie de Medici series.

It is true that the traditional literary practices of *paradox*, *irony*, and *hyperbole*, which have been talked about and so designated from antique literary theory on, bear a kinship to "play" with truth in both means and results. But there is no transfer of those terms to the visual arts over the same time period, or any equivalent usage. And it is not, in any case, until the eighteenth-century that the use of those literary terms can be extended to apply to an outlook or tenor of presentation governing the work *as a whole*, so that the author's own attitude is thereby called into question (e.g., Swift's *Verses on the Death of Dr. Swift*; Voltaire's *Candide* [1759]; Baron Munchausen's *Narrative of his Marvellous Travels*, published as a version of the true baron's adventures by Rudolph Raspe [1789]). These are all instances in which the reader's response is turned inward to the authority, rather than to just the credibility, of the assumed fiction itself.[28] Whereas mendacity may entail merely the embroidering of circumstances and assisting presences in the depiction of an event or ingenious adulation of its subject—so that palatability is thereby increased and per-suasiveness even enhanced—on the other side of the modern, expanded notions of irony and paradox and corresponding forms of "play" with truth there lies, in an extension of the same premises, what becomes, in its manifestations in this century, a deliberately adopted confusion of truth and false-hood. Thus Marcel Duchamp's whole artistic career was gov-

erned by what he once referred to as a "meta-irony": his
remarks and conversations about it were consistently designed
to undercut the seriousness and affirmative character of his
endeavors, thereby suggesting an attitude of indifference.[29]
After ceasing work on the *Large Glass* in 1923, and allowing it
to be believed that he had given up being an artist by not
denying the rumor that was circulating, the activities that he
designated as continuations from then on (machines for optical
experiments, a study of roulette risks, the study and playing of
chess) were deliberately aimed at subverting any clear-cut distinction between what could be counted as art and what could
not. At his death in 1966 it was revealed that he had in fact been
working for twenty years, in complete secrecy, on a final and
summative masterwork (*Etant Données . . .* ).

Duchamp gave to the artifacts that he produced a fasci-
nation, like that attaching to the actions of a spy or agent
leading a double life, by using the relation between creative act
and comment to dress everything that he did in an atmosphere
of insincerity. In *Tu'M* of 1918, his supposed "farewell" to
painting, the objects whose shadows are shown cast on the
canvas surface include two of those he had chosen to exhibit as
"ready-mades," while the third is the shadow of a corkscrew.
Asked by the person cataloguing his oeuvre if the corkscrew
should also count as a ready-made, Duchamp replied no, but
the shadow should count as one.[30] This was to imply that the
trace of an object (painted, in fact) could be substituted for the
thing itself, since it could be claimed as having the self-same
substantive qualities. It was also to draw attention, within the
physical totality of this work, to the difference between the
shadow of the corkscrew—an object not there in the work, *or*
in Duchamp's oeuvre—and the shadow of the bottle brush, an
actual one that is inserted into the painting. In another, very
different example, his adoption of Rrose Selavie as a female
alias originated in a punning inscription that he had written on
one of his friend Picabia's paintings.[31] Later he dressed up in
the part and had himself photographed by Man Ray (fig. 23),
another close associate and one with a strong penchant toward

62

23. Man Ray,
Portrait of Marcel
Duchamp as Rrose
Selavie, photograph,
1920–21. Philadelphia
Museum of Art, The
Samuel S. White 3d
and Vera White
Collection.

the photographing of female subjects. In this act of his, a sexual
play with words was brought to life, absurdly and wittily, yet
also in concrete and transsexual form. Also provided was an
alter ego, substituting for Duchamp's own identity (creative as
well as sexual) rather than actually displacing it; and his later
re-use of the persona combines both of those aspects, as on the
*Perfume Bottle* of 1921. Or to take a third case, different again
(and designedly so), but sharing with the other two a deliberate
insincerity: the *Female Fig Leaf*, in painted plaster, of 1950.[32]
This appears to derive, by the use of a mold as in a life mask,
from the genitals of an actual female—with a corresponding
anatomical explicitness—but was in fact made from the life-
size figure in plaster that became the centerpiece of *Etant
Données . . .* on its completion. Duchamp thus knowingly
provided at that time an accessible trace of an inaccessible
image. It is a "fig leaf" in the sense of physical conformity to
what is masked, but not in the socially conforming sense of a

covering over of sexuality. Colored as Duchamp painted it and placed on display as an object, it presents the most intimate female body part in eminently tactile (rather than just visually recognizable) form; so that Duchamp could have labeled it, like his equally explicit foam-rubber breast of 1947, "Prière de toucher" (Please touch), in contravention of the regulations normally governing works of art or any special object on display in public. In other words, Duchamp works here on the viewer's expectations with both a true and a false derivation of the object and, as the title suggests, both a true and a false availability to the touch of what it represents. The insincerity, then, belongs to both act *and* underlying attitude, and this explains its peculiar and yet extraordinarily provocative force of example.

The use of photographs by Duchamp for such a purpose is particularly suggestive: they stand for, and so are truthful about, what they are literally related to by virtue of a causal physical relationship. Their meaning is in that sense determinate. But of course this is compatible with—indeed it is the very foundation for—the kind of play with truth that we have been describing. Is it, then, specifically modern images, and not those of earlier times, that possess the kind of ambiguity that is in question here? What our examples of visual truth from earlier painting were meant to suggest is that the issue is not that simple.[33] For once we recognize that truth does not entail, now or earlier, simply truth of representation, but that the implications conveyed or beliefs induced by the image are also relevant, then we can see that these issues have not just newly arisen.

To fail to recognize the role played by ambiguity of that sort in Duchamp's case is, we would suggest, to make his practice here, and the kind of interest that his work has recently generated, unintelligible. It is just because he plays off different kinds of truth one against another that his work seems both rich and elusive. Truth in the shape of the "trace" that one has of a particular physical presence; truth as embodied in the implied history of an object like the *Female Fig Leaf*; truth considered in terms of the beliefs induced by the artificial and rhetorical character of a staged photograph: all of these senses of truth are, we want to argue, here interrelated. The narrowly visual sense of truth and the ways in which truth involves what might be called ideological concerns cannot be separated. Photographs, again, are especially felicitous examples, for it is just because of their claims to being true in that more narrow sense that they raise these larger ideological questions.

Analogous to what Duchamp does in those forms, some contemporary advertising images deliberately exploit a confusion of truth and falsehood, because the possibility of "distancing" from the subject that is set up in this way has an amusing and catchy effect, which helps to sell the product. One particular example, chosen for its visual make-up and the associative features (of action, grouping, gesture, and expression) that it embodies, rather than for the relationship of image to accompanying text, may bring out the possibilities that exist here (fig. 24). It is one of a series of advertisements for ladies' shoes and sandals in leather, sold at a smart New York showroom and other fashionable stores. The main visual image (sometimes accompanied by a supplementary one below showing examples of the shoes lined up) consists of a composite or manipulated color photograph, which has the tradename "Candie's" overprinted on it; the name and location of the store appear below, along with a brief verbal indication of the appealing quality of the shoes or their "classic" status.

The basic falsehoods of the image, in this example, have to do with the questionable possibility of young women practicing golf (with a driver) in an indoor space and on a polished surface of the kind shown; with the apparent distance from the viewer of the young man who appears actually making a golf shot, further back and presumably in an extension of the space that the young women occupy; and with how that distance is established. The accompanying coefficient of truth, which allows the viewer's inference or fantasizing to do its work on these falsehoods, is that the poses of the young women have in fact little or nothing to do with golf practice, but everything to

24. Advertisement for Candie's shoes, issued by El Greco Leather Products Inc.

do with the man's presence and their awareness of what it means to them that he is there. Complications and confusions enter into the image as so described, first of all because shoes directly echoing those worn by the young women have a prominent place in the foreground. The form in which each of these shoes is shown is almost completely literal, except that their isolation and angling make them like objects on display, and they appear picking up light and casting shadow against a continuous shining and reflecting surface, which in turn makes the golf balls, spaced like them, seem like candy balls. As for the poses, they avoid the candor of sexual explicitness—while coming close to that—by virtue of the man's appearance in the background and his nominally secondary role. The design is one effectively denying that there could be any connecting bond of that sort between the images, while at the same time invoking the viewer's complicity in what has been done here.[34]

The alert yet disengaged character of the facial expressions
serves as a key to all this. It projects a pattern of behavior in the
young women that is both lively in its attention-getting qualities and governed by savoir-faire. And the evident import of the
advertisement is to associate that combination of qualities and
its effect on the male, who is given a surrogate presence in the
scene, with the wearing of the shoes themselves.

Such examples of the confusion of truth and falsehood are,
then, not simply like showing amongst the victorious leaders
celebrating after a battle a general who had fled dishonorably
in the course of it; the examples are more like giving the man a
pose, expression, and relationship to his fellow generals which
conflicts with his being seen as a brave man and a fine leader. A
similar point might be made about modern novels that in their
make-up include pastiche of expected forms of description, or
disconcerting juxtapositions of modes of writing that entail
quite incongruent and even irreconcilable criteria of believability.

This brings up in a more general way the forms taken by a
"play with truth" in the case of literature, and especially in
statements that occur in literary texts.[35] To establish the appropriate terms of comparison here, we may consider first the way
in which, in a historical or socially oriented novel, the capture
of Moscow, or the character of a real person (such as Queen
Anne), or a morning in the fish market in nineteenth-century
Paris might be described. For a relativist, the truth or falsehood
attributed to the account is a function of what one knows or is
aware of about the actuality in question, put into relation to
one's presumptions and inferences about the person giving the
account. For the structuralist, the apprising of there being a
truth or falsehood to be talked of depends on the novelistic
framework within which particular passages of assertion,
description, and characterization are inserted. And it is of
course true in a very basic, built-in sense that questions as to
what is true and what is false in a work of fiction—however

nominally factual or historical it is—could not be raised without one's taking into account, in both of those ways, the nature of the reader's understanding and the way in which one assimilates such a text. However, the assessment of the "play with truth" that takes place in the works of David, Goya, and Seurat discussed above is more akin, in the considerations that are brought to bear, to the discussion by a "moral" critic (of the *Scrutiny* kind) of what happens in a complex work of literature with a moral tenor to it, than it is to what applies from a relativist or structuralist viewpoint. The account of the Battle of Borodino in *War and Peace*, the characterization of the Duke in *Measure for Measure*, the evocation of the workings of the law in *Bleak House* may all be discussed by such a critic in comparable ways, as richly suggestive elements within a larger literary and dramatic fabric. One *can* discuss "context" and "framework" in the case of those paintings: for example, the showing of the chapel tower struck by lightning beyond the window in the David; the use of landscape elements for scenic background in the Goya; the provision in the Seurat of an outer frame to the painting itself, consisting of dots. But what comes up in such discussion is likely to bring in additional associations or to bear on the creative process, thereby making a supplementary rather than a constitutive contribution to the assessment.

To put the point more abstractly, the "play with truth" in the case of visual images does not operate within a framework of assumptions that narrows or pins down the possibilities of interpretation, as in alternative possible readings of the same textual passage, where the one adopted is context-dependent in the sense of its being tied to a particular place of appearance or situation of linguistic usage. Nor does it operate within a scheme of polarities and dichotomies established in the surrounding framework of presentation, a framework governing, in the case of statements embedded in literary texts, how the words are to be taken. Rather, it operates within, and upon a network of beliefs, presuppositions, and proclivities on the viewer's part. It does so in such a way that consideration of

"frame" and context of presentation may provide an additional
set of associations, or offer insight into methods of working.
But it may more often and more simply be the case that—as
with the text attaching to the dress advertisement and its
appearance in a fashion supplement—frame and context serve
to ratify rhetorically and to direct attention to what is already
implicit in the character of the image itself.

It is just because truth here involves such a framework of
beliefs that the meaning of images is both difficult to pin down
and historically variable. To determine the truthfulness of an
image in this interpretative sense requires pointing out beliefs
and assumptions that, in relation to contemporary images, are
more often implicit than explicit; and, when looking at images
from earlier times, we need to reconstruct the implicit beliefs
and assumptions of those times without simply imposing our
ideas on those people. An altarpiece trades on a different
framework of beliefs than our contemporary advertisements;
and the religious texts illustrated in old master works are
different in both content and effect from the words on advertisements. That altarpiece reminds us of our sins, and "works"
if we fall to our knees; this advertisement is a success if we go to
buy the product. The differences here are not just differences in
visual content. But acknowledging this point need not make us
skeptics about visual truth. Much contemporary literary criticism denies that the meaning of a text can ever be made
determinate. Textual meanings, we are told, are the product of
readers' interpretations; and ultimately we can only compare
and contrast different interpretations without picking out one
as definitely valid. We are not making such a point about visual
images. Indeed, to point out as we have that these images may
be true or truthful in different, perhaps incompatible ways is to
note, rather, an interesting complexity in our notion of truth.
And to seek to compare contemporary with earlier images is to
acknowledge, furthermore, that we can see how these ways of
judging images have changed over time.

We can begin to see here why neither relativist theory of
interpretation nor structuralism as applied to literary discourse

works very well for visual images. Nor do they work very well
for some forms of language either, in the following sense. If
someone says (at the bridge table) "always cover an honor with
an honor," or (of someone's choice to marry an ugly woman)
"you don't look at the mantelpiece when you poke the fire," or
(apropos of how he is dressed) "one ought not to wear a
panama hat after Labor Day," they are enunciating a behav-
orial injunction, or perhaps even a "rule of life" that has come
to be articulated, like proverbs and the precepts of folk wisdom, in this particular linguistic form. The first of these sayings
embodies a leading principle of card play; the second represents a securing in pithy form of the observed fact that sexual
attraction often has little to do with physical attractiveness; the
third designates what has, perhaps somewhat mysteriously,
come to be taken and recognized as an accepted social norm.
They represent in this fashion "truths" which come into everyday life and talk, by virtue of what we have called *excerption*
and *condensation*. But to specify in this way the context of
usage and framework of beliefs that give such statements their
meaning is to say nothing whatever about the force of implication and suggestion that may attach to a particular person's use
of them: they may be implying that this particular case is an
exception to the general rule in card play, making a joke of the
fact that men actually say such things about women, or making
an apologetic response to a compliment on how they are
dressed. It is tempting therefore to treat such cases as these last
as if they were personal variations upon, or deviations from,
the application of the words that is established by their already
existent context and framework of usage. But the problem then
is that the deviation or variation in the use of the words and
what it signifies can only be recognized on internal grounds: by
virtue of the appearance and self-presentation of the person as
they make the remark, and thereby slant or inflect its application. It is a problem substantiated by the divergence that may
well exist, especially in tribal societies, between what people
say that they consider true in the way of beliefs (when asked or
prompted), and what they actually believe.[36]

This is a point that can also be related to the content and format of a literary text.[37] The author or narrator might state there that "Juliet is the sun," and the tradition of poetic discourse and evocative description in literature, along with the character of the passage or context in which the words appeared, would then allow the reader to know or infer that—in contrast to a statement that was to be taken literally as an affirmation or attestation, such as "Juliet is thirteen years old"—this was a metaphorical statement, and hence could not be taken as in itself true or false, but only as apt or inapt to the person referred to, being true or false to her character as delineated. To this extent the understanding of the words "Juliet is the sun" as they occur in a novel and their pragmatic application to the character of that name can be taken as paralleling the real life situation in which a person crossing the road in one's company says "I am looking for a bank where the wild thyme grows," and one is able to infer from the context and framework of conversation that he is not referring to a bank in which to keep his money; or, alternatively, that he is referring to a bank of that sort, but making a joke, which may be apt, about something that is not at all likely to be true of *that* bank in a literal sense. If, however, a character in a novel who is fond of using lines from plays says suddenly and out of nowhere, without any specified object of reference, "I know a bank where the wild thyme grows," only the association that these words carry by virtue of where they come from and the tone given to them in the utterance will enable one to say whether the person is using them to carry a particular implication or suggestion, or simply quoting for its own sake, perhaps because he likes the sound. The words qualify as true or false, as spoken by this particular character, not in accordance with differing interpretations put upon them as the context or format might indicate, but simply on the basis of their being spoken by him in a certain way.

To apply what has been said here about the force of implication and suggestion to visual images once more—some of them earlier, some contemporary—one can understand in this light why a Renaissance representation of Mars in his courtship of Venus, let us say Veronese's (fig. 25), should be regarded as true: because what it shows is not an ordinary or average day in the life of an ancient god, represented in the form of an incident

25. Paolo Veronese, *Mars and Venus United by Love*, c. 1580. The Metropolitan Museum of Art. All rights reserved.

or details from such a day. Rather it conjures up the character of Mars, as transmitted intellectually from ancient times down to the Renaissance and re-interpreted there.[38] Analogously, in the Catherine Deneuve perfume advertisement (fig. 12) a person who already has glamour, in the tradition of cinematic starhood and the context of *Vogue* magazine, is shown in a special moment of appearance such as we might be privy to, presenting herself as if the use of Chanel No. 5 were the key to her charms: a connection that, by a kind of metonymic substitution, we are invited to accept as true. In the nature of the medium, frontality combined with isolation and framing make for a close-up, direct image, as if, looking into a mirror, this is what Deneuve would have seen. And yet the association between the labeled bottle and her features is structurally quite arbitrary.[39] It seems to hang in space beside her, strangely in physical terms and even illogically if one wanted to ask what it was doing there—as it would not be illogical to ask of the Carpaccio (fig. 15) whether the peacock was in fact, as it might be taken to be, standing on the squire's head; or to read the hand position of Mars in the Veronese in relation to the sword taken from him.

One can understand also why in the Western tradition a life or death mask taken in plaster or wax from the features of a famous person (fig. 26) should have a charismatic value attached to it, as evidential record of the person's appearance. To quote from an American publication of 1899, presenting the series "Life Masks of Great Americans" made earlier in the century by John Henri Isaac Browere, such records where they exist "[permit] us to see and know how many of the great characters who have gone before . . . actually looked when they lived and moved and had their being";[40] and the process was such that it could also be supposed, in appropriate cases, that the facial expression was attributable to the pain of having the plaster pulled off. The mask, in turn, might have metal castings made from it which, in a special yet commonly accepted sense, count as "true" portraits of the person. Comparably, the seals of approval that are used for promotional purposes on the outer

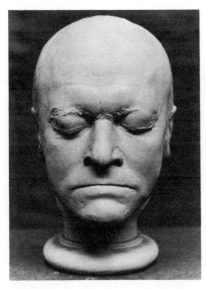

26. Life mask of William Blake, August 1, 1823, made by James B. Deville. National Portrait Gallery, London.

packaging of consumer products such as cereals are both derived from what exists (or did once exist), in the form of an award for merit, and appear to reproduce the real thing. They are usually shown in a nonliteral context which, like the placement of life masks on bases of some sort, emphasizes the schematic character of the usage and makes for a distinctly ersatz effect.

One can understand finally why Renoir's *Moulin de la Galette* (fig. 27) should be accounted "true": not in the way that Constable's *Wivenhoe Park*, with its grazing cows, or virtually any Impressionist landscape can be taken as true, as a record or reproductive representation of a particular place and time of day, from a particular point of view,[41] or in the way that Zola's "Ventre de Paris" might in some parts or elements be descriptively true; but rather insofar as both Renoir and Zola give incarnation to underlying and essential social characteristics of the Paris of their time. Epitomized in the Renoir is a certain bourgeois style of leisure activity and pleasure taking. In a much lighter vein, the images in the Virginia Slims cigarette

27. Pierre Auguste Renoir, *Dancing at the Moulin de la Galette*,
1876. Musée du Louvre, Paris.

advertisements (fig. 14) that photographically conjure up
"moments" in the past when a married woman dared to light
up a cigarette in front of her husband, and the forms in which
she received her equally "period" punishment, work to rather
similar effect. The artificially introduced sepia tones add to the
sense of past social incident, here being preserved in amber;
and along with the written story line there is in this case a
relaxed image of modern woman in color, to make the point
about her having truly "come a long way" in the meantime.

One may—to revert to some of the terms brought up earlier
—contrast those sorts of truth, of a larger or more "generic"
kind, with a more "literal" or specific truth of a visual kind,
based on how things appear. But one does so in the sense that is
illustrated by Nabokov's little poem:

Here, said the guide, was the field,
There, he said, was the wood,
This is where Peter kneeled,
That's where the Princess stood.

No, the visitor said,
*You* are the ghost, old guide
Oats and oaks may be dead,
But she is by my side.[42]

28.  André Kertész, *Chez Mondrian*, photograph, 1926. Copyright André Kertész.

A truth that is distanced by time and is finally spiritual supplants here the truth of mundane and pedantic report.

Much the same could be said of what happens in André Kertész's photograph *Chez Mondrian* (fig. 28), taken in Paris in the 1920s, looking out through the doorway of the artist's Rue du Départ studio. We are shown a worn wooden stairway and its rail, continuing up and past, with strong light falling on the landing and entering the room from that direction; a coat rack on our side of the mat, where planks change to tile, with a straw hat and coat hung neatly on one of its pegs; and a narrow table supporting a vase with a single tulip in it, which has been painted white. In the mood of austerity that the photograph projects, in its patterned structure of coldness and stillness, in its indirect yet powerful evocation of neatness and strictness, aspects of Mondrian's daily life and environment are made to reflect what he was about as an artist.[43] What we are given is true in retrospect, in an extraordinarily distilled sense, to Mondrian's personality and the nature of his work. And it is a truth that (like Zola's) is made present in visual form.

# Chapter Three
## Visual Lying: On the Notion of Falsehood in Art and in Photography

*"Painting is a lie, or most of it is."*

IRIS MURDOCH[1]

ISSELA BOK, IN HER recent book called *Lying*, argues essentially that lying has become more endemic and pervasive in the modern world. Within the terms of her discussion she includes not only "clearly intended" lies, but also "more marginal forms of duplicity," such as evasion, euphemism, and exaggeration, which equally have the aim of disguise or leading astray.[2] How does what she affirms, as a reflection of changing beliefs and moral and social values, apply to the visual images of modern culture? It must be remembered in this regard, that duplicity, as well as being a moral offense, is also—at least when it proves effective—an *art*.

There have in fact been two traditional justifications going back to antiquity for the use of guile and deception in art. The first treats success here as a matter of imitative skills: the result or product has been thereby rendered so real that it was, or could be, taken for the real thing. In antique art theory and again in Renaissance writings about art, this view of the practice of artistic deception applied particularly to still life—as in the famous anecdotes about the rendering of grapes and linen drapery on the part of Zeuxis and Parrhasius—and to portraiture. Alternatively, the image might be seen as so successful in suggesting the possible that it carried the power of suasion. Success here—as in the representation of heroes in action or the illustrious dead—is a matter of the narrative and/or the emblematic conviction that the rendering achieves (the term *emblematic* being used in reference to pose, gesture, attributes of the figure, and other related features of the imagery). Such a viewpoint allows for, and indeed serves to justify, what may be termed a "licensed aliterality" on the artist's part, as in the case of history painting, religious subject matter, or statuary.

The criticism that addresses itself to the nature and achievement of artistic images, rather than simply their miraculousness of existence, operates in antiquity, and again more strongly from the fifteenth century on, according to two corresponding criteria. The first of these is a matter of *correctness* of representation, which is to say accuracy or truth of detail, most often in conformity to an existing text. The second is a matter of the decorum or *appropriacy* of what the artist chooses to do.

In modern aesthetics, in contrast, there is a change of interpretative framework, which carries growing authority from
the late eighteenth century on. The nature or effect of the
change, in regard to representational liberty, is such that things
that artists do, and always did, come to carry negative connotations, in social and political terms. Even the very act of describing and identifying what the image is like and what its realiza-
tion entailed may be slanted and weighted so that it carries such
overtones, which are not at all present in traditional commentary on art, either eulogistic or critical.

To identify how this change happens, a specific breakdown
of "visual lying" is needed. This can be done under three
distinct headings. While overlap may of course take place, and
boundaries in between are left vague so that the same visual
image may be placed under more than one heading, familiar
contemporary examples illustrating each type of falsehood
have been matched in what follows with the interpretation of
works belonging to different centuries and countries, in order
to clarify in both of those ways what the most basic distinctions
are.

First of all, there is fabrication, which is to be understood here
as the creation in visual form of "impossible worlds": for
example, a maze-puzzle in which one finds one's way from
"bottom" to "top" of the buildings depicted using only down-
ward steps. Fabrication of such a kind is basically a selfvalidat-
ing type of deception. We are confronted with the claims of
credibility that the object or product makes; and in rejecting
those claims, we are still at liberty to admire, from differing
standpoints, the artifice that is entailed. In traditional trompe-
l'oeil illusionism, in contrast, the deception persists (at later
viewings) only in as far as the use of the other senses for
verification is denied and a fixed viewpoint is enforced, so that
the sense of miracle or astonishment remains intact.

In Pieter Bruegel's *Netherlandish Proverbs* of 1559 (fig. 29)

29. Pieter Bruegel the Elder, *Netherlandish Proverbs*, 1559.
Staatliche Museen, Berlin, Gemäldegalerie.

pies are shown on one of the village rooftops. At the simplest
level of explanation, elements such as this serve to suggest
(along with others like them in the painting, such as a man
hitting his head against a wall) how the ramifications of human
folly can spread to encompass the whole everyday world. For
the modern art historian Hans Sedlmayr, writing in 1934,
Bruegel's pictorial technique was one that served specifically,
in passages of this sort, to convey the *dis*-relationship—here of
a gravity-defying kind—between objects and their environment.[3] For Bruegel's friend and contemporary Abraham
Ortelius, writing in praise of the artist in 1574, the artist's
representational skill in this kind of effect was an earnest of his
unidealizing fidelity to nature. For Sedlmayr in his later writings, on the other hand, such an "alienation" between the
different components of a work of art became increasingly, in
its modern manifestations, an index of what he termed the
"loss of center" in nineteenth- and twentieth-century art.[4]
Thus the placement of the pies, in their circular dishes, in front
of and against the roof tiles (fig. 30) becomes in this view not

30. *Netherlandish Proverbs*, detail.

simply a means to evoke the degree to which human fantasy is capable of permeating from thought into actuality, but the fabrication of an "impossibility" that directly embodies the artist's sense of what is out of joint in the world.

In moral terms, fabrication is a form of "fakery." In fact, the term *fake* as a designation of behavior only came into being from the late eighteenth century on, and its modern application to visual images is still more recent. Before that, the corresponding term for the production of such artifacts was *counterfeiting*, which could designate a skill or capacity in the maker. So used, it had connotations, like those attaching to any strong imitational ability, of exemplary and even virtuous endeavor. Or the painter could be taken as offering the kind of thing that a mirror image can help to achieve: a literal but at the same time purified form of visual replication.[5] From those points of view, Bruegel could be thought of as literally depicting, in the most convincing fashion, or as rendering in equivalent visual form, the sense of the proverb "The roof is covered with pies" (meaning that overabundance prevails). In neither of those cases would there be any of the overtones that are found in Sedlmayr's account of his art.

The second type of falsehood consists of making things appear as they are not, as for instance in those diagrammatic puzzles where lines are made to appear to diverge, when they are in fact parallel to one another. The best single term to describe, in the most general way, what takes place here is probably the now old-fashioned notion of "dissembling"; and the closest equivalent in current usage may be the notion of "shamming," which comparably carries connotations of disguise or concealment. In the construction of visual images, there may be a cueing of the viewer so that false inferences are drawn, which is a form of disguise, as in the magician's use of misdirection; or internal inconsistencies or contradictions may be left unresolved, so that there is a masking of the underlying situation; or more generally, expectation may be contravened by some intervention of a seemingly arbitrary kind. Making things appear as they are not is not the same thing, accordingly, as making things unrecognizable or indulging in fantasy for its own sake; though either of those two processes could have such an effect.

In an essay of 1907 on Claude Lorrain's art, Roger Fry recorded his difficulty in making a clear-cut distinction between what represented "lucky defect" and what was to be taken as "calculated negation." Referring particularly to the drawings and to Ruskin's characterization of them as looking "like the work of a child of ten" (fig. 31), he wrote that naivetés of composition, which might or might not be intentional, sometimes had "the happiest effect," while at other times they seemed "not childlike but childish."[6] On the assumption that such graphic effects of Claude's represented a masking of his actual technical ability, or a concealment of his acquired knowledge as to how to compose landscape structures, or a contravention of what was normally expected in the way of a complex rendition of space in favor of simplicity, then the impressions thereby given would have to be intended ones: childlike—in the phrase Fry used to distinguish his own perception from Ruskin's—rather than childish. But there is no documentary evidence that posits such an intention on Claude's part.[7] Joachim von Sandrart, writing in 1675–79 and specifically mentioning sketching expeditions that they had made together in the 1630s, says only that the method of drawing that Claude had practiced before their encounter (which took the form of preliminary color sketches or wash drawings, made outdoors from nature) did not suit his talents at all, and he therefore abandoned it, in order better to exhibit his grasp of perspective in painted studies made from nature. Fry's view of how Claude arrived at his naive successes had therefore to be based—as his argument as a whole implies—on consideration of his other drawings, as then known, and inference from the seeming contradictions that they displayed, either internally or amongst themselves.

To be able to claim successfully that someone is dissembling or shamming always depends, in default of a known intention, upon a framework of comparison within which actions and

31. Claude Lorrain, *Nocturne,* drawing, c. 1640. British Museum, London, Department of Prints and Drawings. By permission of the Trustees.

reactions are seen. Fry had his own bases of comparative judgment, including other great draughtsmen of Claude's period and other types of draughtsmanship. While his view remains critically interesting, it is safe to say that no one today who knows Claude's art at all well would subscribe to it; and we can therefore ask on what comparative terms the shift of understanding here has been based. Probably it results not so much from an expanded sense of the function of Claude's drawings or the evolution of his draughtsmanship—since the basic range of his graphic oeuvre was already mapped out by what was available for study before Fry's day—but rather from an increased exposure to how children actually draw, and from a much altered and enlarged sense of the characteristics, both technical and conceptual, that lead to an artist's work being thought of as "naive" or "childlike" in character. Intentional "childlikeness" and deliberate "childishness" are then, from this perspective, quite differently distinguished, and rec-

ognizable characteristics founded on such distinctions come to
be considered as leading to "falsification" of appearances, in a
way that was not at all present in the earlier concept of an
inherited skill or technical practice that is either put to use or
held in abeyance.

The third and final type of falsehood to be considered is
pretense. To pretend may be to lay claim to a knowledge or
skill that one does not possess, and the creative product that
results may then be simply judged as overambitious or unconvincing. Given that an artist is acting sincerely and with integrity, there is no hard and fast distinction between this and
fabrication or making things appear as they are not; they also
can be taken as forms of pretense. But the operative manner in
which pretense, as a deliberate and contrived form of falsehood, applies to visual images is in the form of what can be
termed *as if* representations. In Charles Philippon's famous
graphic demonstration, made up of four sequential images,
Louis Philippe's features are shown as if they were turning into
a pear. Or, to take an example that entails a playful highlighting of behavior, Garrick's wife is shown by Hogarth as if
she were his inspiring Muse, standing behind him in a pose and
pattern of action that implies this.

Arnold Hauser in his *Social History of Art* (1951) saw the
renaissance of pastoral in eighteenth-century French art as
built on what may be called an ethos of pretense: one that,
particularly in the case of Watteau (fig. 32), found its audience
in a courtly society that now responded to the display of
gallantry as a "pure social game." Watteau's first biographer,
Jean de Julienne, in the summary of the artist's life published in
1726–28, had said merely that he worked for friends who
understood his talents, and excelled in *gallant* subjects (among
other genres of work). But for Hauser, the fiction in French
literary pastoral of "fine ladies and gentlemen" indulging in
amorous exchanges in the guise of shepherds and shepherdesses
had already, a century or more earlier, "lost all relation to
reality." That such forms should be revived and reach a peak of
development in Watteau's time he found consonant with the

32. Antoine Watteau, *The Pleasures of the Dance*, 1717. Dulwich Picture Gallery. By permission of the Governors.

"extremely artificial social conditions" in which the upper classes were now living; and with their "no longer believ[ing] in the deeper purpose of those forms," so that the insincerity of the fiction—designed to keep love at a distance—became paramount.[8]

Lovers in Restoration comedy were expected to pretend to one another; it was an operative convention of the time. Nowadays, to convey the corresponding notion of artificiality or dissimulation, one would have to use terms such as *masquerade* or *imposture*, terms that denote the action of laying claim to an identity that is spurious or that bears no relation to social or behavioral actuality. But it is of course also possible for play-acting to be in earnest, and for the art in pretending to take on an identity of its own. A redeeming seriousness may then be seen as working to give depth to the pretense, as in the judgment of Hauser and others on the successes of the rococo; whereas for the imputation of falsehood in the pretense to hold, "as if" representations in art have to be judged, like styles of behavior (such as dandyism), according to a larger social picture of what is barren, escapist, or trivializing.

The negative connotations that have come up, then, in the above survey of how "visual lying" is to be understood, represent or reflect concerns that modern writers have brought to the discussion of earlier art forms, whereas in their own period these concerns carried no such connotations for writers and viewers.[9] In our own time, all three negative connotations have been made to apply to academic art, most especially the "official" art or Salon painting of the mid to later nineteenth century, which goes under one or other of those names for convenience. This art has been held up as an example of everything that painting should not be, or treated as a laughingstock, on three corresponding counts:[10] its totally fictional invention in the realm of subject matter, especially in the attempt to make the past come before one in exact detail; its falsification of appearances, as seen in the way in which the nude female figure is given a constitutionally impossible and purified physique; and its artificiality of convention, as shown in the tenor of pose, gesture, and expression adopted in aristocratic portraiture.

All three of the basic forms of visual falsehood considered— fabrication, making things appear as they are not, and pretense —are also to be found in popular visual imagery, in familiar and widely appealing form, and with no such negative connotations attaching to their presence there. Thanks to a history of many changing adaptations and a sophisticated sense of what can be engendered in the viewer in the way of rapport or a knowing kind of enjoyment, they can indeed be thought of today as built-in aspects of this imagery. Examples, chosen to suggest the responsiveness that such images can evoke in a wide audience, would be: for fabrication, M. C. Escher's logically impossible architectural constructions; for making things appear as they are not, the record cover by Michael Cooper for the Beatles' album *Sergeant Pepper's Lonely Hearts Club Band*, consisting of a montage of heads and costumes making it appear that all kinds of dead people are standing together with the Beatles, to form a crowd; and for pretense, Richard Avedon's group of photographs of Marilyn Monroe, done for *Life* (1958), showing her as various famous film stars, such as Lillian Russell and Marlene Dietrich.

While there need be no open conflict here with the critique of nineteenth-century Salon painting—on the premise that two quite different forms of traffic in visual imagery are entailed, and that the "academic" kind achieved its popularity much earlier than the other kinds—it becomes harder, when these latter kinds of falsehood are accepted without reserve or questioning, to apply the criteria so that academic art is made to seem totally hollow. Those learning about the nineteenth-century may have it instilled in them that this is the way to respond, and it may be in keeping with continuing mythologies about the development of modern art to believe as much; but it is also possible to respond to such images in a less than fully serious way, or in terms of the "change of pace" that they provide. That this can happen now provides an opportunity to look back on the development itself which brought in the modern aesthetic notion of visual falsehood and gave prevalence to a kind of argument that had the chance to flourish.

In explanation of the change here, it might be claimed first that the philosophical framework altered. Metaphor, for instance, in the sixteenth and seventeenth centuries was regarded simply as a trope or figure of speech; in modern times, it has increasingly been seen as a pervasive presence in everyday language, serving to make experience conceptually understandable and to structure events in ways that can be paralleled outside the verbal sphere.[11] And similarly, perhaps, with "as if" representation, something that was available to artists to use as a figurative device turns into a way of structuring and making sense of the way in which an artist "sees" the world as a whole.[12]

A second kind of explanation would be that in the modern

period the traditional genres of art break up, or break apart. In the process of reforming, they become less clear-cut in their categorization then they have previously been, and at the same time, they become more inherently specialized in their appeal. One example that makes this point would be the development of melodrama. Melodrama had always been a feature of theatrical writing and performance: in the modern period it becomes possible to consider it as a modality of presentation available for serious purposes to novelists and, equally, to painters; but it also becomes a particularized form of popular entertainment, with its own built-in conventions. Those conventions play with the exaggerated and the absurd, with the audience's direct connivance. And it could similarly be claimed that popular response to an art such as the Douanier Rousseau's, in which all the objects are made to appear hypertrophied and preternaturally still, was based on a willingness on the viewer's part to suspend disbelief, in response not to the medium in general but to this particular and factitious kind of painting.

Still another form of explanation would focus on the growing democratization of the arts in the modern period. Since the forces at work here enter into all forms of two-dimensional visual imagery—including prints, book or magazine illustration, and posters—and the results of their working permeate throughout society, one of the key functions of fantasy in any form must inevitably be the provision of an escape mechanism, for those who need to step outside the concrete and limited possibilities of their work or life situation. Science fiction illustrations and posters, which deal in the suggestion of impossible rather than possible worlds, would then be forms of fabrication catering directly to such escapist social needs.

When these three types of explanation are put together historically, nobody could question the proposition that from a traditional standpoint (whichever explanation is stressed) the devices used for the embodiment of visual falsehood have become, in their public form, more standardized and homogeneous; while private forms of awareness that transform or question appearances have veered correspondingly toward metaphorical or indirect forms of presentation. But now consider the viewpoint on this historical shift of two writers particularly concerned with questions of illusion and truthfulness, E. H. Gombrich and John Berger.

Gombrich, in the final chapter of his *Story of Art* (1950), suggests that it is a general condition or problem for artists in modern times "not [to be] satisfied in simply representing 'what they see.'" Dali, Picasso, and Klee are taken as each in his varying way reneging on the traditional mimetic aims of art. For present purposes Picasso, in the example Gombrich chooses of a *Head* of 1928, represents fabrication: "he [wanted] to find out how far the idea of constructing a head out of the most unlikely forms could be carried." Klee represents making things appear as they are not, on the analogy of Fry's characterization of Claude's art: "[the look of] a childish scrawl did not worry [him] overmuch. . . . [He] longed to get rid of the standards of earnest grownups and recover the unspoilt imagination of the primitives and of children." And Dali, whose imagery reflects, as compared to an Aztec rain god, "the elusive dreams of a private person to which we hold no key" sets up the impression that there might be such a key: "[he] gives us the haunting feeling that there must be some sense in this apparent madness."[13] In this view, then, these three artists are ones in whom the negative connotations attaching to the three basic types of falsehood are carried to an extreme.

At the same time Gombrich responds warmly to the work of Escher. In photography he is interested in certain devices that can be used for amusing or attention-getting purposes, such as the registration of size constancy, and in arrested facial expressions and gestures of a catching kind. He also appreciates "as if" devices in advertising, such as a chimney made to look as if it were a person reading a newspaper.[14] All these forms of imagery he admires *because* he sees them as communicating effectively; and hence he has been frequently accused of not caring, by comparison, for modern art, and even positively disliking it.[15] His case is much like that of the person referred to earlier, as seeking to respond positively both to immediately likable aspects of popular imagery and to Salon painting. At different levels of seriousness one can find both appealing, but only if traditional standards of mimetic and illusionistic acceptability are being set aside for this purpose.

John Berger's central argument in *Ways of Seeing* (1972), in the sections on the nude and on advertising, combines the idea of tools (even tricks) at the artist's disposal, which can be adapted for particular purposes of falsehood, with the idea of social pressures reflected in visual imagery, which govern the suggestions that are pervasively present in popular visual forms, such as pinups and publicity photographs. The Western European tradition of the nude in art is built, for Berger, around the convention of showing the woman passively look- ing out at a presumed male spectator, who is staring at her nakedness. This is a device that, in the hands of an artist such as Lely (who painted Nell Gwynne for Charles II—and showed her as if she were a Venus accompanied by Cupid), serves to express a woman's submission to the royal owner of both her and the painting. Designed for the express purpose of male flattery, this convention reaches a peak of absurdity in nine- teenth-century academic paintings of nudes, which serve to remind men of state or business that they are men. In pinups and photographs of nude models, the convention becomes standardized, in the shape of the constant implication that the woman "is offering up her femininity as the surveyed." Com- parably, there is a long-standing tradition in oil painting, ac- cording to Berger, of using the combination of poses and gestures (in portraiture), the contents of the setting and an emphasis on materials (as in still life), or both together, to celebrate the ownership of private property. Contemporary publicity images and advertisements take over this visual lan- guage from painting, but with the difference that, in keeping with the pressure exerted by the individual viewer's sense of his or her life within society, there is a play upon anxiety (as to what one does not possess), and the idea of glamour (which is essentially a modern invention and an expression of social envy) is constantly stressed.[16]

To these exposures of falsehood—of falsity to the actuality
of nakedness, in its social function, and to the actuality of what
the working and middle class can hope or expect for itself in a
society that is only nominally democratic—Berger adds, as a
critic writing on twentieth-century painting, the notion of
falsehood to what the artist should be doing, in aesthetic as
well as social terms. It is Klee who becomes here the example of
pretense: one who spent his energies trying to make it appear
that what he did lacked any of the "conscious intention and
deliberate striving" that the spectator should be able to infer
from a work of art. Picasso, again in the role of fabricator, is a
man "who improvises with fragments because he can find
nothing else to build upon." And with Magritte, "the point of
most of his paintings depends on what is *not* shown, upon the
event that is *not* taking place, upon what can *dis*appear," and
the image which consists of five canvasses of parts of the same
woman "proposes that what appears to exist . . . may be seen
as a series of discontinuous moveable parts."[17]
    It is Gombrich's and Berger's introduction of a discussion of
photography alongside, if not integrated with, the discussion
of painting, that is particularly provocative. There is no doubt
that people feel uncomfortable at the juxtaposition of the two.
Such a juxtaposition is in many ways traditional, but the
photographs used in those ways have been ones that had the
look of being art, or that made one think of painting or fine
prints in subject and rendition; whereas this is not the case with
these particular photos from the world of the scientific text-
book, magazine illustration, or advertising. It would seem that
photography in its popular forms poses in the sharpest possible
way the idea of a price to be paid—in the manipulation of
responses—for its power and accessibility; against which is to
be set what a contemporary pluralistic society can endorse—
without any evident struggle—in the way of "falsehood."
    One can try applying the modern aesthetic terminology of
rebuke for falsity (and corresponding praise for veracity) to
photographs of the past, by analogy with painting and prints,
or on the assumption of kindred aims and functions. This is the
way in which the genre and anecdotal subjects of Henry Peach

Robinson and Oscar Rejlander have been traditionally looked upon, the argument being that photography was here "perverted in a mistaken attempt to rival painting."[18] It is also the way in which John Thomson's photographs from the 1870s of street life in London can be criticized, i.e., on the grounds that the images do not show the amount and clarity of detail that would later become mandatory, by analogy with the standards of painting, in confrontational images of contemporary social conditions. And Berger's way with twentieth-century photographers whom he admires is to praise, conversely, those images that single themselves out as corresponding to a realist or neorealist notion of truthfulness: works by Paul Strand and August Sander, which entail a "deliberate, frontal, formal" stance toward their subjects, and one by Rodchenko, which looks very much like a Courbet.[19]

But the way in which all sorts of visual images, and especially photographs, are received and understood today seems to make the criteria in question either old-fashioned or casuistical. One might ask why one should bother with them any longer, except for the purposes of consciousness-raising. This is essentially where Sissela Bok ends up on the subject of verbal falsehood, with its traditional terms of censure and its seeming ubiquity in our own day.

The need, then, is for a new start in understanding how photographs communicate—as distinct from other kinds of visual image, and expecially paintings. Some scattered insights and beginning formulations on this subject have been provided by a few writers, such as Barthes, Bourdieu, and Sontag; but a central framework is lacking.[20] This framework should encompass what Gombrich likes in photographs and the way in which he is able to use them in relation to his argument about painting; and what Berger dislikes in the practice of photography, particularly its commercialized versions, and what he singles out as exceptions.

Our modern aesthetic framework for the judgment of truth and imputation of falsehood, now two centuries old, may raise pertinent questions as to what comes about in the media of film, television, and video: how and why fabrication, falsification of appearances, and pretense may be given apparent trustworthiness there, by the addition of words or the use of voiceover commentary. But it is no good at all for understanding how photographs communicate themselves, as a particular and at the same time ubiquitous kind of visual image. It is also no use for the comprehension of what is now often referred to as postmodernist art, including transmogrified versions of the practice of painting and sculpture, and also forms of conceptual and performance art that entail the use of photography or film, or photographic documentation. In both cases the notion of truthfulness or falsehood and how it is received and recognized appear to be due for redefinition once more.

*Photography never lies: or rather, it can lie as to the nature of the*

*thing, being by nature tendentious, never as to its existence.*

ROLAND BARTHES[21]

In order to establish the framework for a revisionary theory as to how photographs can be subject to the charge of falsehood, it is necessary to begin with the basic distinction (irrespective of medium) between literal images—already introduced into the discussion in chapter one—and ones of a nonliteral kind. To simplify by eliminating the consideration of color and markings such as those made by brushwork, the distinction may be formulated by way of the following examples.

In a drawing or a black-and-white print any particular element of the presentation becomes nonliteral through the way it is placed upon the sheet or seen against the surface of the page. In particular, it may be placed or seen there in collocation with other elements; or in such a fashion that it seems to exist in its own environment of space and atmosphere; or as if it formed part of some larger presentational undertaking (which may explain what is left out).[22] Examples of nonliteral graphic imagery would be, accordingly: botanical and zoological drawings, in which different plants or insects might be combined, set into an invented context, or shown spaced out yet as if coexisting simultaneously; notations of unusual costumes or states of dress (rather than reproductions of the fabric pattern from which they are made, which would also be informational, but in the way that a tailor's swatches are); and anatomical studies of particular body parts (rather than the "cuts" or outline illustrations of the same parts that are placed in a dictionary for definitional purposes).

To those kinds of imagery, in turn, one can contrast—now in terms of the processes or techniques that are used to generate the image—the literal "mapping" of the shape of a person's hand, created by laying it flat and moving the pencil between the fingers; or, in print making, the use of a technique that allows the surface appearance and "feel" of a particular substance to be transferred directly (as in brass rubbing) onto the surface of the work sheet. In these last two cases, one is dealing with the generation of an image that can be considered true or false, since what is said about it ("This is A's hand"; "This, in the print, is the front page of yesterday's *Times*") can comparably function as a verifiable or falsifiable claim to knowledge.

Now a photograph could serve as the basis for an image that was true or false in this latter way. It might, for instance, serve as the basis for the outline illustration in a dictionary, showing what a "gallop" is, in which case it would be giving authority to that illustration, by virtue of being available to testify to its validity.[23] Or, in the example given of a "direct transfer" process, it might form part of the image that was so generated, which would be the case if the page or piece of newspaper used was one that included a photograph. But it would not thereby carry any warrant of its own truth or falsehood.

The processes or techniques used to generate nonliteral images, in contrast to those just specified of a "mapping" or "transfer" kind, are processes that are best described by the use of the generic terms *excerption* and *condensation*, which were introduced in chapter two. The function of excerption, inasmuch as it entails a singling out and detachment of certain elements or materials from reality (as distinct from others), is to bring to the viewer's attention a particular focus or emphasis. That of condensation, representing as it does some kind of a presentation in compressed form, is to give to the image an evocative quality, or resonance, that causes one to search in one's memory.[24] Nonliteral images that are so generated may be true or false in the same way that prophecies, or the precepts of folk wisdom, may be. That is, they can have a quality or propensity to them that is adjudged true or false, in terms of its effect on beliefs. And the quality in question possessed by visual images is likely to be an intended one, like that possessed by relics on display in churches, and the propensity is likely to take the form of a power over the viewer.

A literal photograph would be one that was taken by a mechanically regulated process, such as one that opened and closed the camera shutter automatically at intervals; and a succession of images of this sort would show, let us say, that a certain bank, within which the camera was set up, was or was not robbed, at any particular moment within the time span covered. But the uses normally made of photographs— whether by original design or as a consequence of what they turn out to show—bring up the matter of the relationship of image to text. A photograph that happens to have been taken so that it "catches" a person falling from a fire escape may be used to reinforce dramatically what a newspaper text says about the fire in question; or a photograph of a horse at the gallop may serve to establish on the basis of one single image in a total series—as Muybridge did by publishing such images in a form explaining what they showed—that all four feet are in fact off the ground at some point. But it is also possible that a literal photographic image should be turned by the text to a nonliteral purpose, as when a photograph of a volcano before it erupted is captioned (as if it represented that mountain as it normally or literally was) to go with a story about the eruption. To say which is also to say that the relationship of text to image to accompanying story may inflect the way in which such an image is read.[25]

A photograph that is or becomes nonliteral, by virtue of
excerption and condensation, has three distinct possibilities
built into it as an image—other than the reinforcing of what
the accompanying text is designed to do—which bear on the
sense or senses in which it may be adjudged false. The first of
these is that, in the recording of events, what is shown may not
be what took place, in the sense of any actual portion or
segment of that, but rather an alternative version or re-enact-
ment, both paralleling the event itself and making reference to
it. This is what often and even characteristically happens in the
photographing of rituals and ceremonies. There, the crystalliz-
ing of implications that are latent in the event or the conveying
of its nature in epitome may bring up considerations of decorum and appropriacy, like those traditionally given attention in
the case of painting and sculpture; and the participants may be
asked to assume fitting positions at a separate time or go
through what they did again for the camera, in order that what
the ritual or ceremony may be said or felt to assert is in fact
asserted, in a kind of willed denying of contingency or a re-
sumptive regarnering of what the event represented.

As distinct from the representation of a riot on stage or the
depiction of a historical event such as the Oath of the Tennis
Court (see fig. 19), in which actors or studio models are
accepted as stand-ins, but in common with what distinguishes
the use of documentary footage from a restaging on film,
falsehood here consists of an inauthentic substitution of any
kind. It is of course possible for substitutes to be used deliberately for outrageous or disconcerting purposes, as in trumped
up "news" stories about film stars and politicians. In these
cases, once the inauthenticity has been revealed, what was
done will come to seem droll or bizarre. But there are also more
ambivalent moral questions arising from the fact that coopera-
tive subjects are at the will and disposal of the photographer, to
do what he or she wishes with their appearance and behavior.
For instance, Frances Benjamin Johnston, working for the
Hampton Institute in Virginia in 1899, showed the families of
blacks who had graduated from the institute living a material,

33. Frances B. Johnston, *A Hampton Graduate at Home,* photograph, 1899. Courtesy of the Library of Congress, Washington, D.C.


spiritual, and domestic life of order, tranquillity, and harmony (for example, saying grace around the table at Sunday dinner, fig. 33), in images deliberately created to contrast with ones in which blacks of Virginia, who had not had the same ¹ucational benefits, were shown living a life of poverty.²⁶ And again, there has been discussion recently of whether, amongst the photographs that Walker Evans made in the later 1930s of Alabama sharecroppers, the one of a family to whom he was close which shows them as they wanted to be seen, all posing for him by their cabin in their Sunday best (fig. 34)—a photograph that Evans suppressed in the sense that he put the negative aside without making any print from it—is in fact "truer" to the human character of the different family members and their relation to one another and to their physical environment than the images that were chosen to accompany James Agee's

34. Walker Evans, *A Sharecropper's Family, Hale County,
Alabama,* photograph, 1936. Courtesy of the Walker Evans Estate.

text describing the poverty of the same people, *Let Us Now
Praise Famous Men,* which was published by the two in 1941.
Alongside this there also goes evidence indicating that Evans,
in photographing the household of another family, chose to
make rearrangements for his purposes in the placement of the
furnishings, some of which are equally described in Agee's
text.[27]

The second possibility relevant to truth or falsehood that is
inherent in a photograph is that it can seem to literalize an
intervention into actuality on the part of its subject, either
putative or desired. Thus a photograph taken from the hatch of
an airplane can imply a gravitational pull or accelerated thrust
down toward earth, which seems to carry both the camera and
its holder along with it; and a pair of hands that are shown in
the air, or in empty space, can appear as hands that are actively
engaged in doing something, or that aspire to be so engaged. To

make clear what is particular to the medium of photography
here, as compared to paintings and prints, there can be, just as
in those media, a cropping or cutting down or cutting through,
which gives special status to a part or fragment. There can be
excision or insertion, and these can serve as processes of
amendment, as in the reworking or restoration of pictures.
Collage techniques or combination printing can equally be
used, as vehicles of fantasy, and there can be doctoring and
tampering which can serve to make things unrecognizable,
with roughly the same kinds and extents of tolerance for such
processes as with modern and abstract art. But what sets the
photographic image apart is above all its own particular quality of "transparency," giving it a kind of "thereness" that life
could never have. The sufferance of falsehood is, then, wished
upon the viewer—in the "literalizing" capacity of the medium

35.  Philippe Halsman, *Dali Atomicus*, photograph, 1948. Courtesy
of the Halsman Estate.

102

36. Harry Shunk, *Yves Klein, The Painter of Space Launches Himself into the Void*, photograph, 1960.

in general—by the creation of a conflict between that transparency, and what is possible or believable. Thus Philippe Halsman's well-known photograph *Dali Atomicus* (fig. 35) used a very high shutter speed to make it appear that the furnishings of the studio, cats, water from a bucket, and the artist himself are all flying through the air simultaneously. In as far as the result appears both astonishing and convincing in its defiance of gravity, it is to be judged as a brilliantly audacious piece of "trick" photography. Or again there is a photograph, issued as a postcard (fig. 36), that purports to show the artist Yves Klein projecting himself from an upper story above a Paris street. The claim made on the viewer's beliefs by what is literalized here is not only curious in its falsehood, but becomes entertaining in that what is literalized is an aspiration to intervene into actuality, in a way that would make the impossible come true. And in fact it first appeared as the frontispiece to an imitation newspaper of the artist's (1960), advertising himself as "The Painter of Space Launching Himself into the Void."[28]

The final possibility to be considered is that a photograph may entail putting on view not the person who forms its subject but the playing of a role that is assumed, assigned, or discovered for the camera. Thus in the nineteenth-century practice of photographing stage personalities in the studio in their well-known roles, the presentation is one assumed to fit with what the public for such images expects, or to conform to its stereotyped patterns of recognition. In contrast to paintings that imply a particular viewpoint for the spectator and offer an engagement of the presentation with that viewpoint, but in common with the practice of fashion photography, the presence and focus of the camera serves in such cases as a theatricalizing agent, from the point of view of public consciousness.[29] The moral problem attending such photography is that the image may seem self-serving, in its enhancement of what is already, or underlyingly, an assumed role. Falsehood here occurs, correspondingly, because the photographer makes a suggestion by the use of the camera for which he or she may not want, and does not have, to assume responsibility. Some erotic photography can be charged with failing to take responsibility, but the social and political implications that attach to such a charge are made clearer in the accusation brought by Susan Sontag against Leni Riefenstahl's book of photographs of a Sudanese tribe, *The Last of the Nuba* (fig. 37). The Nubans are

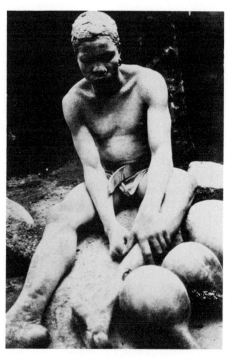

37. Leni Riefenstahl, Wrestler in meditation on the day of initiation, color photograph. From *The Last of the Nuba* (New York: Harper and Row, 1974).

shown, according to Sontag, as a "tribe of aesthetes." They are made to act out the role of "almost naked primitives [who], awaiting the final ordeal of their proud, heroic community, frolic and pose under the scorching sun." And the underlying purpose of this, as the accompanying text makes clear, is to "whitewash" Riefenstahl's prior involvement with Nazi ideology, by rewriting in this form the larger themes of her cultural past.[30]

Those three possibilities of the photographic image are also ones that have been exploited, in more self-questioning and reflexive ways, in the fields of conceptual and performance art.

For instance, the use of the photographic image there for the purpose of documentation, from the later 1960s on, includes cases where it serves to testify to the actuality of what was done, or to the outcome of what took place, in the shape of a record of an apparently straightforward kind: as when Joseph Beuys included in an exhibition of his life and works a photograph showing himself as a dive bomber pilot during the Second World War, standing beside his plane (fig. 38), and identified this as having been taken after a forced landing in the Crimea, where he records that he was cared for by the Tartars, after being hit by Russian gunfire and bringing his plane down behind the German lines.[31] Or the photograph might serve as the residue, or replacement, of an intervention into actuality. This was purposefully intended by Robert Smithson in his work of 1968–69 entitled *Nine Mirror Displacements in the Yucatan*, inasmuch as the photographs that he published (fig. 39) of these arrangements of pieces of mirror in different spots give little or no indication of scale and almost none of sur-

38. Joseph Beuys after forced landing in the Crimea, photograph, 1943.

39.  Robert Smithson, *Nine Mirror Displacements in the Yucatan,*
1968–69, photograph showing second displacement. Copyright
Nancy Holt. Published by New York University Press.

rounding environment. In addition, as he recorded in his
accompanying text, the mirrors were removed so that, quite
apart from the difficulty of finding the sites again even with the
aid of his map system, only "memory traces" of what he had
done would in fact be left there.[32] Again, in performance art
of the 1970s, the photograph could be used, in the form of
projected slides, to create a superimposition of "live" and
"screened" elements or a blurring of the distinction between
the two. Or the fact that what was done was performed before
the camera, or as if it were, might serve to ritualize or theatri-
calize an event (or nonevent), in the form of stills deriving from
it (fig. 40), or corresponding images that served like a form of
self-display and self-advertisement.

Such uses of the photographic image could be described as serving to generate a kind of "metatruth" or "metafiction."[33] The quality of truth or falsehood can in principle be attributed to them, on the same cognitive bases as the photographic images discussed earlier; but only suppositionally. For the viewer is asked to accede to their belonging to a "world," or province of creation, which legitimates questions as to what is true and what is not, in parallel to the real world from which they derive; but also one in which what is "real" and what is contrived as fiction is not subject to accreditation in the same kinds of way as there.

What happens in recent art works of those kinds may seem very abstruse, but it links back to a common understanding of what truth and falsehood mean, and the nature of that understanding as reflected in language, in the following way. When crea-

40. Cindy Sherman, Untitled study for film still, photograph, 1980.

tions, products, or forms of self-display are being discussed in everyday terms, to say that something is false commonly carries one or more implications of a particular sort. The choice of the word may designate an artificial or synthetically composed version of the real thing (as with false eyelashes); or it may give notice of features that cannot be simultaneously consistent with one another (as with a false note in a musical performance) and perhaps are deliberately contrived not to be (as with a false harmony); or, finally, the falsity may define itself in opposition to what are considered "true" values, of a social and behavioral kind (as when one speaks of people giving themselves false airs).

The positive claims that can be made on behalf of falsehood in modern visual imagery are likely to be, correspondingly, those of enjoyability; an intendedly superficial appeal, which masks out faults beneath the surface; and a quality of visionariness that (nevertheless) comes through. While photographs may naturally be thought of as displaying these qualities, without too much scrutiny or concern as to why, it is obvious from what was said earlier that an art that actively flaunts its nature from these points of view will elicit strong reservations, if not outright hostility, from those who hold a commitment to traditional pictorial values. Yet at the same time those qualities and their flaunting are the basis for the growing authority and appeal that Marcel Duchamp's example (see fig. 23) has come to exercise over the last twenty years.

What the Duchamp legacy means—as embodied in the uses made of photographs, and also of schemata, shadows, or imprints of objects in counterpoint to the real thing—is that in postmodernist art the application of the notions of truth and falsehood comes to be, at the least, more variable and of a more empirical kind. The nature of the work may cause what is true or false to become completely indeterminate, or to seem that way: a point which, in a conceptual piece, may extend to accompanying information, that is itself under the artist's control. Or the indices of truth and falsehood—insofar as they can be established only on the basis of what is seen to occur in the act or performance itself—may in some performance pieces become totally self-referential. In some photographic work in series, which has hovered intermediately between being considered as experimental photography and being taken as postmodernist art, the same is equally true.[34] In short, one must be prepared, in the 1980s, for much more of all those things, and the framework for the understanding of what "visual lying" entails can be expected to shift also, to assimilate these changes.

To end with a prognostication, then: as the relation of visual images to the world of reality that we accredit changes in its workings or gives the appearance of doing so, so also certain concepts that have long been central to the recognition and evaluation of art will shift and accommodate themselves in their application. One of these concepts will be originality, taken as the capacity to arrive at an image (or set of images) that has the potential of appearing true insofar as it is quite unlike the work of any other. A second will be invention, understood as entailing the capacity to depart from literal representation toward metaphorical or suggestive implications which carry the personal stamp of the exercise of imagination or fantasy on the part of their originator. Finally, the idea of intellectual or ideological "comment" in visual form will change equally, even if it be essentially playful or facetious in spirit—and perhaps most of all when it is that. In these differing ways, the appraisal of artists' works in terms of the falsehood they offer, or the kind of falsification they indulge in, will be no longer tied in the sense that it has traditionally been to the function or "intention" of images.[35]

# Chapter Four
# How to Analyze Truth and Falsity in Visual Images: Some · Concluding Suggestions

*The philosophical understanding of "truth" in aesthetic contexts is at least as obscure as is the case for symbolism.*

MARY HESSE[1]

I N THE THREE PRECEDING chapters we have provided a wide
range of examples of visual truth and falsehood and made
suggestions about some conceptual frameworks in which
those examples might be placed. This is not, we are sure, the
right time to propose any very rigid framework, for an attempt
to pigeonhole images by placing them in strict categories of any
sort is certain to be quickly undermined by further consideration. In the preface we indicated how we want to treat theory in
relation to examples, but such theories can become a positive
liability if not sufficiently flexible to accommodate new examples and new conceptual approaches. Now, having adduced
our examples, it might be useful, first, to indicate some of the
directions in which we anticipate new research to develop, and,
second, to present a tentative summing up, a statement drawing together our current thoughts about the theory of truth and
falsehood in visual images. Three areas deserving attention and
exploration might be cited.

As the selection of our examples is intended to indicate, one
fruitful avenue for ongoing research is relating contemporary
and popular imagery to the traditions of visual art. The working assumption of our book is that any hard and fast distinction
between serious and popular imagery is surely unsatisfactory.
So, a good theory of visual truth must draw together our ways
of thinking about old master and modernist, "serious" and
"lowbrow" art. Here Meyer Schapiro's pioneering essay
"Courbet and Popular Imagery" (1941), recently republished,[2]
anticipates much current work, and some concerns within the
contemporary art world as well. We become aware that while
the distinctions between such popular images and how they are
transformed by a serious artist are important, an interesting
analysis of visual truth must account for both kinds of representations. Furthermore, in the period during which we have
developed this study, much of the best-known contemporary
visual art has been concerned with taking up and transforming
such popular imagery. Much of the debate now going on about
neo-expressionism invokes claims about the truth or falsehood
of such images. For political artists like Leon Golub, a number

of German painters, and a more established figure like R. B. Kitaj as well, such concerns about truth are especially pressing. Their aim, as politically motivated painters, is to tell the truth about our society. How is that goal to be achieved in visual form?

Another fruitful avenue, to which our examples are also intended to contribute, lies in exploring the attempt of art historians to reflect critically on the history of their own discipline. Today a study of eighteenth-century French aesthetic theory is of more than purely historical interest because the debates of that time over how images may be properly called truthful relate to current art.[3] To write a history of art at all, it is perhaps necessary to deploy some notion of visual truth. At least, whether we are dealing with Vasari's notion of art as a compellingly deceptive illusion, or Gombrich's sophisticated development of that claim, art historians have long tended to organize the materials of their study naturally in terms of some such conception of truth. Of course, we may also talk about being true to the materials of art, or to the spirit of a historical period; and the attempt to discover what is living and what is dead in such discourse constitutes a focus of study in itself.[4] As art historians continue now to develop such studies, we anticipate other attempts to work out an analysis of truth of images. What will be most fruitful, we mean here to suggest by our own form of argumentation and practice, is an account that both presents an interesting viewpoint or vantage point on traditional art theory and offers a multitude of examples.

Finally, and this area is the most difficult to define, what is also relevant in our account is much within contemporary philosophy and literary criticism that is not explicitly concerned with visual images. When, for example, a distinguished philosopher of science like Hilary Putnam says that "the idea that truth is a passive copy of what is 'really . . . there' has collapsed,"[5] we see how current debates about scientific truth are relevant also to truth in pictures. Other important philosophers—Nelson Goodman and Arthur Danto, for example—have explicitly linked their general philosophical programs to accounts of art; and the contrast of these approaches to that of

Richard Rorty, whose latest book now relates American to French and German philosophy, is only starting to be developed.[6] As this debate proceeds, it would be desirable that people interested in visual art be prepared to evaluate critically this work in another discipline, and apply it.

At the end of the epilogue to his great study of narrative, *Mimesis*, Auerbach explains the difficulties of writing such a book without a good library. He then adds: "On the other hand it is quite possible that the book owes its existence to just this lack. . . . If it had been possible for me to acquaint myself with all the work that has been done on so many subjects, I might never have reached the point of writing."[7] We, happily, have a different problem; so much work on our topic is already accessible, and more material is appearing so rapidly, that it is possible now to write only a tentative account. Acknowledging, then, the inevitable limitations of this study, how can we synthesize the material we have presented? Here is a possible framework, a sketch for what we call a system of symbolism.

If the claims that people make about truth and falsehood in visual images, and the corresponding opinions that they hold, are to be drawn together and collectively reviewed, it must be with the awareness that any such attribution of truth or falsehood to a particular image will be necessarily and contingently affected by (1) prevailing ideas regarding the medium and its development over time; (2) the form in which the visual image is physically or presentationally contextualized (in a book or magazine, on a museum wall, and so on); and (3) presuppositions or preconceptions on the viewer's part concerning the intent of the artist, or the corresponding communicative function and force of the image.

Given those varying backgrounds to conventional discourse on the topic of truth and falsehood, this means that there will be a strong element of personal choice in each individual's use of different conventions of response, according to the kind of visual image to which he or she is most inherently attracted and the way in which it is described and (either in interjectional form or in more socially prescribed language) appreciated. There will also be conventionalized forms of categorization on which to fall back, the most familiar (and perhaps the most enduring) of which is the division of visual images into those that are instances of "realism," in that they represent or record the "real" in some directly responsive and therefore potentially truth-telling or falsifying way; and those that are instances of "symbolism," in that they are imaginative and indirect in approach and entail a corresponding use of culturally codified symbols. And, finally, there is likely to be an available and often popularized mythology regarding a particular artist and his endeavors, or, in the case of essentially anonymous works, artistic endeavors belonging to a particular period and place.

The purpose of what follows is not to refine upon those conventions or to redefine their scope, but rather to summarize in semiotic terms how the attribution of truth and falsehood to visual images operates within a "system," concentrating for this purpose on the most basic oppositions and distinctions built into it.[8] What is thereby created for questions of truth and falsehood is a system of symbolism, which is unlike the conventional (and necessarily arbitrary) dichotomy of realism/symbolism referred to earlier in that it extends the notion of symbolism (or symbolicity), in line with current sociological and anthropological usage, to embrace the generative and communicative processes as a continuous and unfolding whole. The term *symbolism* serves in this way to designate how particular kinds of "signs" come to operate as they do in visual imagery, and what happens to them in the process.

We can begin then by distinguishing the underlying conditions governing the generation and reception of visual images from whatever interpretative conventions may be imposed upon them; or, to put the same thing another way, we distinguish the actual conditions of nonverbal discourse *through* images from the trappings of verbal discourse *about* them. In recapitulation of what was said in chapter one about the application of those conditions to the attribution of truth or falsehood: a visual image may be considered true, or come to seem that way, insofar as it is taken:

(1) as embodying a certain quality or effect. This means that certain features have been singled out for emphasis—given "iconic" status—as opposed to others.

(2) as evidentially securing that a happening or process took place. The image serves here as an "index" of that event or process, as opposed to indirect evidence being relied upon.

(3) as summing up and showing forth certain social and political values. Here the doing of this opposes itself "symbolically" to the creation of an image which is "opaque," rather than "transparent," in the values that it shows forth.[9]

The basic terms for the processes by which potentially symbolic visual images are created, brought up in chapter two and used further in chapter three, are *excerption* and *condensation*. Excerption, understood as the singling out or detachment of certain elements from reality so that a particular focus or emphasis is given to them (p. 47), may entail in practice a sharpening or playing down of features or materials that are apprehended in terms of their truth or falsehood. Condensation, representing a presentation in some kind of a compressed or distilled form, may work similarly through expressive refinements, indeterminacies of context, or intercalibrated associations to trigger evocatively, through the search in the memory that is set up, a sense of what is true or false.[10] A *literal* image is in general, as set out in the opening chapter, one that has not—or not yet—been subjected to such processes. Though they are somewhat unusual, each medium or basic category of visual image will have its own illustrative examples (pp. 16, 96–97).

In the "play with truth" discussed in chapter two, a second-degree version of those processes comes into operation. Either there is a displacement of attention from other aspects of the captured scene that would normally appear as of equal or greater importance (second-degree excerption); or what is already an iconic or tableaulike kind of image becomes imaginatively embellished by the artist's total means (second-degree condensation); or already schematic forms of representation are combined for the purposes of evoking a larger typicality (a combination of the two).

The ascription of falsehood to visual images discussed in chapter three does not simply represent an inversion of the above scheme, or its negative counterpart. It rests on three possible claims or charges being made concerning the character of the image, each of which is given a distinctly negative connotation: (1) that of fabrication, as opposed to the showing of what does or could reasonably exist; (2) that of making things appear as they are not, as opposed to the way they are or would seem to be; or (3) that of pretense, as opposed to sincerity, honesty, or some equivalent term.

In photography (pp. 98–104) the "play with truth" leads to the imputation of falsehood being made on the grounds of (1) inauthentic substitution, (2) the creation of a conflict between the "transparency" of the photographic medium per se and what is possible or believable, or (3) the making of a suggestion for which the photographer does not take or assume responsibility. The oppositions in these cases are obvious ones, and again intrinsic to the nature of the medium.

What is said here about the "system" pertaining to photography applies also—in terms of deliberate confusion of truth and falsehood, rather than mendacity (pp. 59–60)—to some advertising using photography, and to some conceptual and performance art (pp. 64–66, 104–7).

Though the word *system* is used here, our aim has not been to put forward any fixed scheme of analysis, but rather to provide a framework for ongoing and no doubt ampler discussion. Concern with the truth of images relates to many concerns that are proving currently of strong interest. These include the status of photography as an art; arguments about the rhetoric of new wave or transavant-garde painting; discussions of semiotic approaches to old master art; and feminist critiques of erotic imagery. It falls within our purview to suggest some ways of linking together those concerns, and others related to them, and to contribute to or influence thereby that ongoing discussion.

These are only some of the questions now relevant. Film raises similar problems, as debates in newspaper columns and even in popular periodicals suggest. Is the Australian film *Gallipoli*, though uncannily accurate in its topographical and military detail, one that plays false to history, in presenting a picture of the climatic assault that is slanted to bring out its purposelessness, and is in fact gravely misleading in its larger suggestion as to what war then was like? [11] Is *The Deerhunter* untrue because its central motif, the playing of Russian roulette, presented as a sadistic device of the Vietnamese which then becomes part of the lives of the American soldiers even after they return to Saigon, is in fact literally untrue; or does that motif capture the situation of those soldiers truthfully in a metaphorical sense? Is *Absence of Malice* misleading to the point of untruthfulness because it describes in ways that are not true to fact the position of a district attorney, and probably the workings of an investigative reporter also; or does this literally fictional framework give a sense of how the press may actually possess a power in excess of its due?

It seems indeed to be inherent in the character of visual images that they should put different sorts of truth into conflict with one another in such ways, and to do so may in some cases be an essential premise of their workings. While this book was being completed, we saw Rainer Maria Fassbinder's film *Lili Marleen*. This is a nice example with which to close our account, for it raises all the major issues about systems of symbolism on which we have just touched. It represents a fictional story, in its cast of characters and what happens to them, but it is one that is built around true facts about the history and popularity of the song "Lili Marleen." It has a plot that entails the confusion in people's minds of the person who sings the song (who she is, why she sings it) with the actual

heroine of the story, and the manipulation of both for propaganda purposes. It is visually presented so that the "real"
parts—war scenes at the front—seem deliberately artificial,
and the "fictitious" parts, such as the rallies at which the
heroine sings the song, are rich and striking in their command
of political and social detail. Thus it is a film that deals with
truth and falsehood within a symbolic system, sometimes
separately, sometimes side by side, and sometimes in confusion
with one another, and so to try to encapsulate what makes for
truth and falsehood here without first defining the subject and
describing the cinematic structure would be totally impossible.
It is also a film that could be said to "deconstruct" what
happened in the history of the song; and it is a film that is
pregnant correspondingly with the truth and falsehood of
social and political relations.

One reviewer we read found this film deeply puzzling. Did
the trenches *really* look like that, he asked; and how could the
man who loved Lili Marleen have learned to conduct Mahler
symphonies? If one leaves aside the element of simple and
somewhat comic naiveté here, these can be taken as potentially
interesting questions applying to a great variety of visual
images. How can a truthful film or depiction of contemporary
events be made? Is it relevant, for example, that the actor
playing the hero of *Lawrence of Arabia* looked very different
from that figure, or irrelevant that the star of *Gandhi* is an
Indian actor? Can we compare a sixteenth-century *Last Supper*
depicting that event as a contemporary banquet scene with an
attempt by Poussin to reconstruct the setting in what he thought
were archeologically accurate terms? In what *differing* senses
might all these art works be called truthful, and what can we
infer about the mental attitude or disposition of the viewer who
judges them truthful? Here, again, we see how complex our
attitude is toward truth of art works, and how difficult it is to
indicate exactly how we find them truthful, while knowing that
ultimately they are merely fictions. It is to those kinds of
possibility in visual imagery that we have addressed ourselves
in this essay.

# Notes

Chapter One
On the Nature of a True Visual Image
and How to Find One

1. *Soliloquies* 2.10 (18), cited in *Fathers of the Church*, vol. 44, trans. H. A. Gilligan (New York, 1946). We are indebted for our awareness and understanding of this passage to David Summers, who drew our attention to the place given to it in his book (Summers, *Michelangelo and the Language of Art* [Princeton, 1981], chap. 2).

2. "The *truth* of these charming works instantly strikes and delights us ... M. Constable ... is as truthful as a mirror. I only wish the mirror reflected a magnificent site like the mouth of the Valley of the Grande Chartreuse near Grenoble" ("The Salon of 1824" in *Stendhal and the Arts*, ed. David Wakefield [Phaidon, 1973], pp. 109–11).

3. Alfred Dauger reviewing the Salon of 1851. This and the passages that follow on the *Stonebreakers* are taken from T. J. Clark, *Image of the People: Gustave Courbet and the Second French Republic, 1848–1851* (London and New York, 1973), p. 145.

4. Letter to Francis Wey, late 1849, cited in Clark, *Image of the People*, p. 30, but in a translation that is modified for present purposes.

5. Advertisement in *Le Peuple*, June 7, 1850; cited in French, in ibid., pp. 162–64.

6. See the account of his reaction in *L' Evénement*, March 11, 1866 (ibid., p. 135). For a valuable theoretical and philosophical review of the mid- nineteenth-century uses of the word *truth*, see James H. Rubin, *Realism and Social Vision in Courbet and Proudhon* (Princeton, 1981), chaps. 8–9.

7. For the Toulouse-Lautrec placed amongst other images of the dancer (some of which also show her in the Fire Dance), see Margaret Haile Harris, *Loie Fuller, Magician of Light* (Richmond, Va., 1979).

8. For correspondence theories of truth applied to pictures, see Theodore M. Greene, *The Arts and the Art of Criticism* (Princeton, 1940), p. 424, and the further discussions of John Hospers, *Meaning and Truth in the Arts* (Chapel Hill, N. C., 1946), chap. 6; Kingsley B. Price, "Is There Artistic Truth?" *Journal of Philosophy* 46 (1949): 285–91; Louis A. Reid, "Art, Truth and Reality," *British Journal of Aesthetics* 4 (1964): 323–31; and Edward S. Casey, "Truth in Art," *Man and World* 3, no. 4, (1970): 351–69 (with additional bibliography).

9. The alternative to a correspondence theory of truth offered by the writers cited in n. 8 can be considered a coherence theory, insofar as they attribute to

works of art the affording of an insight into reality or experience that has validity—the work being capable of serving compellingly as a source of such insight through the intermesh of its components with salient characteristics of the subject itself.

For a convenient setting out of these two different theories of truth and their contrast to truth considered from a "pragmatic" standpoint, see Donald S. Lee, "Truth in Empirical Science," *Tulane Studies in Philosophy* 34 (1966): 45–92.

10. The extraordinary degree of change that perception tolerates here, without diminution of the power of recognition, is scientifically attested to by experiments that include the processing of paintings. The physiological and psychological reasons for it form a fascinating but quite separate subject.

11. For a comparative exposition of the views of the two leading advocates of such a theory with respect to pictures, see David Carrier, "Perspective as a Convention: On the Views of Nelson Goodman and Ernst Gombrich," *Leonardo* 13 (1980): 283–87 (which includes a full bibliography).

12. The recent discussion by Linda Nochlin ("Van Gogh, Renouard and the Weavers' Crisis in Lyon: The Status of a Social Issue in the Art of the Later Nineteenth Century," in *Art the Ape of Nature: Studies in Honor of H. W. Janson*, ed. Moshe Barasch and Lucy F. Sandler [New York, 1981], pp. 669–88) of a drawing by Paul Renouard for a wood engraving of this kind (published in the French magazine *L' Illustration*, Oct. 1884) shows how characterization of such a technique and way of working assimilates itself, in the case of social subjects, to the assumption of authenticity of response: she writes of how "the drawing is rich in the kind of graphic detail that seems to guarantee 'documentary' authenticity," and of a "larger authenticity of the image . . . generated precisely by its concreteness and the modesty of its goals" (p. 674).

Nochlin's article belongs amongst a spate of recent reconsiderations of the phenomenon of Realism in nineteenth-century art, which bring out the great variety of pictorial vocabularies, from country to country as well as decade to decade, that were used to convey a reportorial content, having to do with contemporary events or the state of the world at the time. See on this point the illustrations brought together in "The Realist Tradition: French Painting and Drawing, 1830–1900," exhibition catalogue, Cleveland Museum of Art and Brooklyn Museum, New York, 1980–81, and in *The European Realist Tradition* (Proceedings of 1980 Symposium at Cleveland), ed. Gabriel P. Weisberg (Bloomington, Ind., 1982).

13. Versions, all of 1963, include the *Lavender Disaster* (reproduced in Rainer Crone, *Andy Warhol* [New York, 1970], no. 332), the *Orange Disaster*, and the *Triple Silver Disaster*. Identification of the chair is given by Calvin Tomkins, *Off the Wall: Robert Rauschenberg and the Art World of Our Time* (New York, 1980), p. 262.

14. This example was suggested by Leslie J. Olsen, Department of English, University of Michigan.

15. See Mark Roskill, "On Realism in Nineteenth Century Art," *New Mexico Studies in Fine Arts* 3 (1978): 5–12, which stresses the basic issues of definition here and treats art and literature in parallel, with earlier references brought together for this purpose; and also, for internal criteria of assessment in the case of the novel, George Levine, *The Realistic Imagination: English Fiction from Frankenstein to Lady Chatterley* (Chicago, 1981).

16. F. W. Nietzsche, *Die fröhliche Wissenschaft, Nietzsches Werke,* vol. 5 (Leipzig, 1895): especially, *Scherz, List und Rache,* no. 55, quoted by E. H. Gombrich, *Art and Illusion: A Study in the Psychology of Pictorial Representation* (New York, 1960), p. 86.

17. Stanley Fish, *Is There a Text in This Class? The Authority of Interpretive Communities* (Cambridge, Mass. and London, 1980), p. 241. See also pp. 197–98, where Fish uses what J. L. Austin had said (*How to Do Things with Words* [Oxford, 1962], p. 142) about the context as well as the circumstances in which one might say that "France is hexagonal" to argue that "it is only in relation to 'dimensions of assessment' [Austin's term] that judgments of truth and falsity . . . are possible." For the characterization of Fish as a relativist (though he denies being one), see the review by Richard Wollheim "The Professor Knows," *New York Review of Books,* Dec. 17, 1981, pp. 64–66, where mention is also made of other forms of audience theory that comparably "institutionalize" the notion of literature as entailing the reading and study of texts.

18. Hubert Damisch, "Eight Theses for (or against?) a Semiology of Painting," *Enclitic* 3, no. 1, (Spring 1979): 1–15 (originally published in French in *Macula* 2 [1977]: 17–23); the quote is from the opening statement. The argument is comparativist in that Damisch goes on to advocate the study of a series of works of a certain kind (tableaux, frescoes, decorative ensembles) to reveal a "system of signs," and relativist in positing that the constitution or nonconstitution of the signs "into a system" results from the "attempts" of what can only be individual viewers, focusing on examples that are accessible to them to be so constituted. For the implications of this for art historical study, see also his "Semiotics and Iconography," in *The Tell-Tale Sign: A Survey of Semiotics,* ed. T. A. Seboek (Lisse, The Netherlands, 1975), pp. 27–36.

19. The only recent philosophical discussions of fictional representations and depictions covering both art and literature are those of Kendall Walton ("Pictures and Make-Believe," *Philosophical Review* 82, no. 3, [July 1973]: 283–319 and "Points of View in Narrative and Depictive Representation," with commentary by Marcia Eaton, in *Nous* 10, no. 1 [March 1976]: 49–61). See also H. Gene Blocker, *Philosophy of Art* (New York, 1979), chap. 5, sec. 3, "Truth," dealing mainly with "fictional entities" (pp. 233–45), and Nicholas Wolterstoff, *Works and Worlds of Art* (Oxford, 1980), pt. 7 (esp. p. 357).

20. According to the way in which the word *symbolic* is used here and later, *any* context would in principle have this effect on a literal image (whether or not the representation of which it formed part was intended literally, or was

124

taken literally by its viewers). Clarification of such a use of the term *symbolic* is to be found in Dan Sperber, *Le Symbolisme en général* (Paris, 1974), trans. as *Rethinking Symbolism* (Cambridge, 1975). See esp. the critique there of Vincent Turner.

21.  As Stephen Bann points out in his "Abstract Art—A Language?" in *Towards a New Art* (London: Tate Gallery, 1980), pp. 136–37, Tatlin's *Monument to the Third International* has been turned into a literal image, as an emblem for New Left Books that draws on the political connotations of that tower. It is helpful to think here also of how a mental image may very well be literal: consisting of itself and only itself, devoid of any context and un-associated with any other image; and how one can then "adapt" that image without change to a particular context of appearance, on instruction to do so.

22.  The structuralist terminology of "signs" yields problems here. The basic Saussurian distinction between *signifier* and *signified* obviously works for cave paintings of bison or hearts on trees, so that there the analogy with verbal "signs" succeeds. It is difficult, however, to maintain alongside this the division of visual images, originated by C. S. Peirce, into three sign-types: *symbol, icon,* and *index*. The reason for the difficulty is that in the visual arts one has signs becoming symbols, and icons becoming symbolically (or suggestively) charged, so that they mediate between different spheres of life or con-sciousness; and that this should happen appears to be embedded in the very nature of the genetic and communicative processes in and through which visual images are generated. Rosalind Krauss, who had earlier introduced the Peircean division of sign-types into her critical writings, more recently ("In the Name of Picasso," *October* 16 [Spring 1981]: 13–20) has argued that the "system of signs" in Picasso's Cubist collages is to be grasped and interpreted in a strictly Saussurian basis; but without saying how the Peircean sign-types would apply from part to part or element to element in those works.

23.  In bringing up the roles of negation and synonymity in verbal expression, we do not wish to imply that either or both of these constitutes a determinant way of specifying the basic differences that exist between the verbal and the visual. As against the arguments of Sol Worth ("Pictures Can't Say Ain't," *Versus* 12 [1975]: 85–108, reprinted in his *Studying Visual Communication,* ed. Larry Gross [Philadelphia, 1981], pp. 162–84) which led him to specify that "True-False criteria cannot be applied to pictures" or "pictures be treated as meaningful on a dimension of truth and falsity" (pp. 174, 179), a visual image could have the effect of a negation, in leaving a general out of a battle that he actually fought in, or in showing in place of an art object recognizable as such the accumulation of dust under glass in a gallery. Equally, two different traffic signs, like two different injunctions not to park on a street, can be taken as completely substitutable for one another. And even if those cases are considered exceptions or put in a special class, to attempt to specify differences in such a way is like attempting to specify the differences between what one

perceives (in the real world) and what a visual image shows. There is no single way of encapsulating those differences that at the same time takes account of the correspondences; yet the larger or generic sense in which they differ remains (in practice) clear. See on these subjects, *Imagery*, ed. Ned Block (Cambridge, Mass. and London, 1981)—mainly on mental images—with an introduction that summarizes the major issues. If there is to be a description or elucidation of the differences of some larger sort, it would be in terms of "natural" and "symbolic" forms of discourse about the world—our engagement in it and with it.

24. Whether a literal representation is taken as one that is so intended, one that is so perceived, or one that just "is" will depend on how the act of showing forth is understood. Saint Augustine's examples are the imitations of actors, mirror reflections, and the "brass cows of Myron" (the Greek sculptor), which cover all three alternatives.

25. As set out now by Dennis Porter, *The Pursuit of Crime: Art and Ideology in Detective Fiction* (New Haven and London, 1981), chap. 2.

26. This comment of Cunningham's is printed alongside *On Mount Rainier I* (1915) in the exhibition catalogue, Imogen Cunningham, *Photographs 1910–1973* (Seattle, 1974), p. 34.

27. See most recently, for a summary of all the available evidence here and a review of earlier interpretations, the exhibition catalogue *Edouard Manet and the Execution of Maximillian* (based on the Boston version), Brown University, Providence, R. I., February–March 1981, with essays by various hands.

28. For example, the contention of Nicos Hadjinicolaou (*Histoire de l'art et lutte des classes*, trans. as *Art History and Class Struggle* [London, 1978], chap. 13, "Positive Visual Ideology") that David's *Oath of the Horatii* "embodies a conception of beauty and virtue with which a whole social class identified for a time" (p. 138).

29. See on this point John Fekete, "On Interpretation," *Telos* 48 (Summer 1981): 5–25, esp. p. 23 (citing a similar view taken by Frederic Jameson).

30. T. J. Clark, in his study of Courbet (see n. 3 above) and in his introduction to the companion volume, *The Absolute Bourgeois: Artists and Politics in Nineteenth Century France* (London and New York, 1973) may be taken as advancing a claim that is, at least very generally, of the first kind; for the second alternative, see esp. the presentation by Richard Wollheim, "Criticism as Retrieval," in his *Art and Its Objects*, 2d. ed. (Cambridge, 1980), suppl. essay 4, pp. 185–204, which explores the general implications of the problem in a most illuminating way.

31. See Arthur Danto's recent discussion of this, *The Transfiguration of the Commonplace: A Philosophy of Art* (Cambridge, Mass., 1981), pp. 163–64.

32. "Two Plays" and "Duse and Bernhardt," *Saturday Review* (London), June 1895; reprinted in *Dramatic Opinions and Essays*, 2 vols. (New York, 1906), 1: 124–52 and in *Our Theatres in the Nineties*, 3 vols. (London, 1932), 1: 146–50. The opportunity for these remarks was provided by the fact that, in the same month, Duse was appearing in London in Dumas's *La Femme de Claude* and both she and Bernhardt were playing, at different theaters, Marguerite in *La Dame aux Camellias* and Magda in Sudermann's *Heimat*. I am much indebted for my knowledge and understanding of this passage to Robert Garis, who used it in his *The Dickens Theatre: A Reassessment of the Novels* (Oxford, 1965), chap. 1, "Style and Theatre."

33. Walter Benjamin in his discussion of the Trauerspiel or allegorical drama of the baroque period paralleled visual imagery and theater on what appear to be related lines, in writing that "the function of baroque iconography is not so much to unveil material objects (by presenting the essence implicitly 'behind the image,' as in medieval exegesis of theological symbolism) as to strip them naked" (*Ursprung der deutschen Trauerspiels* [1928; enl. ed., 1974], trans. John Osborne as *The Origin of German Tragic Drama*, intro. George Steiner [London, 1977], p. 185 and see also 222–23).

34. See, for instance, Linda Nochlin, *Realism* (Harmondsworth, 1971), pp. 31–32, which affirms that the Manet offers by comparison "no sense of the confrontation of a climactic moment of truth." Also compare Fred Licht, *Goya: The Origins of the Modern Temper in Art* (New York, 1979), chap. 7.

35. Walter Friedlander, *Caravaggio Studies* (Princeton, 1955), p. 213, cat. no. 39, gives the relevant details. The painting was commissioned by a local magistrate. S. J. Freedberg, *Circa 1600: A Revolution of Style in Italian Painting* (Cambridge, Mass. and London, 1983), pp. 72–77, characterizes it as one of the late paintings of Caravaggio's that in an absolute and simple "unstaged" way appears psychologically and emotionally true.

36. In contrast to the now classic essay of Enrique Lafuente Ferrari (*El dos de Mayo y los fusilamientos* [Barcelona, 1946], trans. as "Goya—The Second of May and the Executions," in *Goya in Perspective*, ed. Fred Licht [Englewood Cliffs, N. J., 1973], pp. 71–91), which rests its argument for Goya's modernity here on the claim that "events are depicted with passionate immediacy, with a total and unadorned surrender to a pure impression of observed or imagined truth" (p. 73), interpretation has been deepened by the visual comparisons or associations that have been introduced since. See esp. E. H. Gombrich, "Imagery and Art in the Romantic Period," *Burlington Magazine* 91 (1949): 153–59, which has been reprinted in his *Meditations on a Hobby Horse and Other Essays in the Theory of Art* (London and New York, 1963), and in Licht, *Goya in Perspective*, pp. 152–61 (comparing British propaganda prints of the Napoleonic massacres in Spain); Folke Nordstrom, *Goya, Saturn and Melancholy* (Stockholm, 1963), pp. 172–84 (referring to the Passion of Christ—an argument that is to be extended in light of probable allusions that

are present to Rembrandt's prints and to paintings of his that must somehow have been known to Goya); Nigel Glendinning, "Portrait of War," *New Society*, March 19, 1970, p. 476 (comparing a print by Gonzalez Vélasquez of the same subject); and, most recently, Jan Bialostocki, "The *Firing Squad*, Paul Revere to Goya; Formation of a New Pictorial Theme in America, Russia and Spain," in *Art the Ape of Nature*, pp. 549–58.

37. See the article by Janet Malcolm, "Maximilian's Sombrero," *New Yorker*, July 6, 1981, pp. 91–94, extending Nochlin's argument (cited in n. 31 above) in order to claim that "it is the invented and imagined Goya that has the greater sense of actuality. The 'truthful' Manet is unconvincing and unmoving," and also referring to the material on Manet's use of photographs brought together by Aaron Scharf (*Art and Photography* [1968; rev. ed., Harmondsworth, 1974], pp. 66–75). The occasion for this piece was the exhibition "Before Photography: Painting and the Invention of Photography," Museum of Modern Art, New York, May–June 1981, with catalogue by Peter Galassi. In the introduction to that publication, an earlier suggestion of John Szarkowski on this matter of "contingency" was developed, but mainly in regard to early nineteenth-century landscape paintings and oil studies of an informal kind. Photographs of public events having such a quality are in fact not at all common before the 1880s, though they are occasionally found, e.g., the recently discovered daguerrotype of the Chartist Meeting at Kennington in April 1848, and also a few images from the American Civil War. Such comparisons as can be made are suggestive of a larger parallel between the differing media to be considered here—including prints—rather than a direct interaction.

38. Differing kinds of argument that have been put forward for there being a culturally or critically relevant kind of shift in the character and structure of narrative painting from the mid-eighteenth century on include, most recently, those of E. H. Gombrich ("Action and Expression in Western Art," in *Non-Verbal Communication*, ed. R. A. Hinde [Cambridge, 1972], pp. 373–93), referring to Hogarth and Victorian anecdotal pictures (pp. 391–92); Ronald Paulson (*Emblem and Expression* [London, 1975]), on later eighteenth-century British art; Michael Fried (*Absorption and Theatricality: Painting and Beholder in the Age of Diderot* [Berkeley, Los Angeles, and London, 1980]), on French Salon art of the same period, linking up with his earlier writings on Thomas Couture and on Manet; and Norman Bryson (*Word and Image: French Painting of the Ancien Regime* [Cambridge, 1981], chap. 8), on David in contrast to Greuze. It should be noted that, in proposing a particular turning-point leading into the modern period and its modes of representation, all these arguments—while extremely interesting in the observations they put forward—tend to imply a lack of any parallel before that time for the type of image they single out as asking to be read in a certain way, and that they also tend to discount the existence of a more popular level of response to visual

imagery, in which the forms of awareness that they invoke evolved more slowly and gradually.

39.  Even if it were the case that both of these alternative claims could be made equally of a particular image—as Gombrich holds to be the case of the Hellenistic representation of the Battle of Issus, known through a Pompeian mosaic copy (*Art and Illusion*, pp. 136–37)—it would not follow that both kinds of truth were to be found simultaneously.

*Chapter Two*
*Painting and Advertising:*
*The Force of Implication and Suggestion*

1.  *Les Maîtres d'Autrefois* (1876), trans. Andrew Boyle as *The Masters of Past Time: Dutch and Flemish Painting from Van Eyck to Rembrandt*, ed. H. Gerson (London, 1948), p. 183 (on the *Night Watch*).

2.  The details that follow are ones brought together and discussed in Theodore Reff, *Manet: Olympia* (London, 1976 and New York, 1977), see esp. chap. 2, pp. 47–59 for the Titian comparison; and in Timothy J. Clark, "Preliminaries to a Possible Treatment of the Olympia in 1865," *Screen* 21, no. 1 (Spring 1980): 18–41, which deals esp. with the responses of critics.

3.  Arthur Danto in his *The Transfiguration of the Commonplace: A Philosophy of Art* (Cambridge, Mass., 1981), uses both these examples in chap. 7, "Metaphor, Expression and Style," pp. 168, 194, to make a point that might be paraphrased not in terms of metaphor as he discusses it but by saying that Saskia is shown fetchingly, Hendrickje is shown warts-and-all. He also uses as examples Cézanne's portraits of his wife and Mantegna's *Dead Christ*, examples that we have adapted for our own purposes.

4.  Manet may have been appealing to an awareness of the power and influence of such courtesans in high society, which is reflected in their portrayal in novels and plays of the time; but when such literary precedents and parallels as exist here (discussed by Reff, *Manet*, chap. 3) are taken as buttressing the claim of the *Olympia* to being comparably a "statement of truth" on the subject (Linda Nochlin, *Realism* [Harmondsworth, 1971], p. 203), the argument risks becoming circular.

5.  Such photographs were first brought into account by Gerald Needham, "Manet, 'Olympia' and Pornographic Photography," in *Woman as Sex-Object*, ed. Thomas N. Hess and Linda Nochlin (*Art News Annual*, 38 [New York, 1972]), pp. 81–89. He treated them, however, as source material for Manet. For photographs that, like the one reproduced here, are in fact much closer in their imagery, see also *Nude Photographs 1850–1910*, ed. Constance Sullivan (New York, 1980), pl. 12 (by Braquehais, c. 1856, it shows the upper half of the body turned round and the head looking out); and Gisèle Freund,

*Photography and Society* (Boston, 1980), p. 73 (by an unknown photographer, it shows clothes hanging up and on the bed and drapes on the wall behind, dirty soles, and a coy expression). See also, for the "dynamic" of what Manet did in relation to conventionalized presentations of femininity, Eunice Lipton, "Manet: A Radicalized Female Imagery," *Artforum* 13, no. 7 (March 1975): 48–53.

6. As in Peter Wollen's reply to T. J. Clark, "Manet: Modernism and Avant-Garde," *Screen* 21, no. 2 (Summer 1980): 15–25. Clark in his rejoinder in the next issue (seriously misprinted) noted that he had now revised his piece on the issue of nudity for its appearance in book form. See also Charles Harrison, Michael Baldwin, and Mel Ramsden, "Manet's 'Olympia' and Contradiction," *Block* 5 (1981): 34–43, where the argument is continued in very dense theoretical terms.

7. Such a relational view of metaphor can be taken to parallel the way in which Paul Ricoeur, comparing the literal and metaphorical meanings of words from an interpretative standpoint, writes of a "nascent" or "emergent" quality to metaphor that links "local events" in a text to the import of the work as a whole ("Metaphor and the Central Problem of Hermeneutics" [first pub. in French, 1972], *New Literary History* 6 [1974]: 95–110, reprinted in Paul Ricoeur, *Hermeneutics and the Social Sciences*, ed. and trans. John B. Thompson [Cambridge, 1981], pp. 165–81). A point made by Stephen Orgel with respect to poetry which is relevant to what will be said later is that the relation that metaphor proposes between the identity of different things can, from the seventeenth century on, no longer be conceived of as in any way "real," but becomes instead purely poetic and fanciful ("Affecting the Metaphysics," in *Twentieth-Century Literature in Retrospect*, Harvard English Studies, no. 2, ed. Reuben A. Brouwer [Cambridge, Mass., 1971], pp. 241–42).

8. Mary Hesse, in an as-yet-unpublished paper, has recently formulated a comparable view with respect to linguistic metaphors and their role in science.

9. See on this subject the analyses of Judith Williamson, *Decoding Advertisements* (London and Boston, 1978) from which this example is taken, and, also, for the implications and intimations of advertisements, Jean Baudrillard, *Le système des objets* (Paris, 1968), pt. 3, on publicity (esp. pp. 196–97, comparing belief in it to a child's belief in Santa Claus), John Berger, *Ways of Seeing* (London, 1972), sec. 7, and Gillian Dyer, *Advertising as Communication* (London, 1982).

10. Taken from the exhibition catalogue "Paris-Paris 1937–1957," Centre Georges Pompidou, Paris, May–Nov. 1981.

11. Roland Barthes, *La chambre claire: note sur la photographie* (Paris, 1980), trans. as *Camera Lucida* (New York, 1980), pt. 2.

12. John Berger, "In Opposition to History, In Defiance of Time," *Village*

*Voice*, Oct. 8–14, 1980, pp. 88–89; taken from his book on photography, developed in collaboration with Jean Mohr, *Another Way of Telling* (New York and London, 1982).

13. The supposition of there being such a sect takes its inspiration from the comparable "Royal Albert Society," dedicated to the memory of the prince consort, that Robert Graves describes having helped found at Osborne in 1917 (*Good-Bye to All That* [1929; rev. ed., London and New York, 1957], chap. 23).

14. References on these points are to be found in *Cérémonies et Rituels de la Maçonnerie Symbolique*, ed. Robert Ambelatin (Paris, 1966), which has diagrams published to go with the 1824 ritual; J. M. Roberts, *The Mythology of the Secret Societies* (London, 1972), pp. 52, 346; and Cynthia Truant, "Solidarity and Symbolism among Journeyman Artisans: The Case of Compagnonage," *Comparative Studies in Society and History* 21 (April 1979): 214–26. The Vuillard is entitled *In Bed* (1891).

15. See the exhibition catalogue, "Old Master Paintings from the Collection of Baron Thyssen-Bornemisza," International Exhibitions Foundation, Washington, D.C., 1979–81, cat. no. 6 (entry by Allen Rosenbaum) for the details referred to. The identification of the figure as a portrait of Francesco Maria della Rovere was made by Roberto Weiss in the catalogue of the Carpaccio exhibition held in Venice in 1963; it may be noted that the presence of the stag had suggested previously that it might be Saint Eustace (so identified in iconographic tradition).The date of 1510, revealed by cleaning, is not absolutely certain, since there is room for further Roman figures that may be missing.

16. See, for the various opinions that have been put forward, A. Bredius, *Rembrandt: The Complete Edition of the Paintings*, 3d ed., rev. by H. Gerson (London, 1969), p. 551, no. 52, and, for the latest interpretation (with a summary of earlier ones), B. J. Brous, "The 'O' of Rembrandt," *Simiolus* 9 (1971): 150–84.

17. On this painting, see Michael Fried, "The Beholder in Courbet: His Early Self-Portraits and their Place in his Art," *Glyph*, Johns Hopkins Textual Studies, no. 4 (1978), pp. 85–129; he refers to these details but discusses the relation of the figure to the space and to the viewer in a much more encompassing, phenomenological framework.

18. See Norbert Lynton, *The Story of Modern Art* (Ithaca, N.Y., 1981), p. 284, remarking on how what "seemingly doesn't matter" is made to matter in this way. The received idea that a creative artist is incapable of repeating himself is to be found affirmed in Edgar Wind, *Art and Anarchy* (1963; rev. ed, London, 1969), beginning of chap. 5, "The Mechanization of Art."

19. The evidence on the subject, literary and visual, is discussed and interpreted in this way by Sir Ernst Gombrich, "Giotto's Portrait of Dante,"

*Burlington Magazine* 121 (Aug. 1979): 471–83. For prevailing conceptions of truth in ancient portraiture, as they may be (very hypothetically) reconstructed from extant Greek and Roman examples, see James D. Breckenridge, *Likeness: A Conceptual History of Ancient Portraiture* (Evanston, Ill., 1968), esp. fig. 49 (portrait of Socrates) and p. 152 (on the Roman Republican tradition).

20. See Discourse 4 (Dec. 10, 1771): *Discourses on Art*, ed. Robert Wark (New Haven and London, 1975), pp. 70–72, 140.

21. Jules David, *Le peintre Louis David, souvenirs et documents inédits* (Paris, 1880), pp. 344–46, reprinted in David and Guy Wildenstein, *Documents complémentaires au catalogue de l'oeuvre de Louis David* (Paris, 1973), no. 1293. The earlier documentation of 1790–92 also appears there; for the evidence as to how David worked on the project, see Virginia Lee, "Jacques-Louis David: the Versailles Sketchbook," *Burlington Magazine* 111 (1969): 197–208, 360–69.

22. Sir Kenneth Clark, *The Romantic Rebellion* (New York, 1973), claims that she has inscribed his name in the dust. The stay on the estate, with which he associates the work, came after the death of the duke in June 1796 and was over by early 1797 at the latest, which was probably when the creation of the *Caprices* began. On the imagery of the suppressed plate, see Francis D. Klingender, *Goya in the Democratic Tradition* (1948; new ed., New York, 1968), p. 90, with further details. E. du Gué Trapier, "Only Goya," *Burlington Magazine* 102 (1960): 158–61, describes the cleaning of the portrait (in the late 1950s) which revealed the *Solo* (damaged) in addition to the *Goya* signature.

23. Meyer Schapiro, "Seurat and 'La Grande Jatte'," *Columbia Review* 17 (Nov. 1935): 9–16, now reprinted in his *Modern Art, 19th and 20th Centuries* (New York, 1978), pp. 101–9, remains the basic discussion of the social and sociological aspects. See also Mark Roskill, *Van Gogh, Gauguin and the Impressionist Circle* (London and Greenwich, Conn., 1970), chap. 3, with additional bibliography.

24. See the review and explanation of the tradition here in David Summers, *Michelangelo and the Language of Art* (Princeton, 1981), pp. 41–55, 104–11.

25. See Walter Friedlander (*Caravaggio Studies* [Princeton, 1955], p. 108) who notes that what Caravaggio does here may reflect the practice that was current in wealthy Roman households at the time of dressing pages in such costumes.

26. See S. J. Freedberg, *Painting of the High Renaissance in Rome and Florence*, 2 vols. (Cambridge, Mass., 1961), 1: 529–30 (Pontormo, Cosimo de' Medici, 1518), from which derives the comment on "suspension" below; and Federico Zeri, "Rivedendo Jacopino del Conte," *Antologia di Belle Arti* 6 (1978): 114–21 (*Portrait of a Man*, Palazzo Bianco, Genoa, possibly by Jacopo before 1535). Cases of "deliberate archaism" are also to be found in the North

in the early sixteenth century, as in the work of Jan Gossaert, Joos van Cleve, and, most especially, Quentin Metsys's *Money-Changer and His Wife* (1514), where the point seems to be to give the painting an old-fashioned, "precious" look. Examples of allegorical portraiture that entail an assumed identity include Cranach the Elder's *Cardinal Albrecht van Brandenburg as Saint Jerome* (version in his study, c. 1525, Darmstadt, Landesmuseum, and also one in a landscape setting). But since such practices have never been focused upon in the discussion of Northern painting, their import is hard to evaluate from case to case. Iris Cheney and Craig Harbison kindly drew out these examples from their respective areas of study and provided references.

27. See S. J. Freedberg, *Painting in Italy 1500 to 1600*, Pelican History of Art (Harmondsworth, 1971), p. 338, on the Sala dei Fasti Farnesi: "Taddeo's artistic forms and aesthetic conceits try to summon from the past an authority more than they intrinsically have; the historicism is in accord with the thematic burden of the room that justifies, by an account of history, the present state of the Farnese family."

28. For the changing connotations of the term *irony*, turning it into a distinct and critically recognized literary mode in the course of the eighteenth century, see esp. Norman Knox (*The Word "Irony" and its Context, 1500–1755* [Durham, N.C., 1961]), who cites and summarizes earlier considerations of the subject. Amongst many recent discussions of the issues posed by the Swift poem, see esp. Irving Ehrenpreis, "Meaning: Implicit and Explicit," in *New Approaches to Eighteenth-Century Literature*, Selected Papers from the English Institute, ed. Philip Harth (New York, 1974), pp. 150–53, and the comparable points about it made by Claude Rawson, "The Rhimer's Recoil," review of A. R. England, *Energy and Order in the Poetry of Swift, Times Literary Supplement*, Sept. 4, 1981, p. 1017.

How the same kinds of thing enter into eighteenth-century art, as well as the literature, might be brought out by a consideration of Watteau's Pierrot and Gilles subjects (for paradox), Greuze's sentimental vignettes of the 1760s (for irony), or (for hyperbole) the emerging tradition of the "sublime"; or, for examples that might be more specifically seen as anticipating the forms of "play with truth" discussed, one might cite the representation of places with significant contemporary events going on in them, developments in associative portraiture and the depiction (before 1790 also) of social gatherings. But since there has been little or no discussion to date of cases that might contribute to a larger argument here, the parallel in the case of art can only be adumbrated.

There have been attempts to find analogous regulatory principles at work earlier, as in the suggested use of the term *bluff* for the writings of Rabelais (Barbara C. Bowen, *The Age of Bluff: Paradox and Ambiguity in Rabelais and Montaigne*, Illinois Studies in Language and Literature, no. 62, University of Illinois, 1972) or, in the case of painting, the application of the notion of paradox to Velasquez's *Las Meninas* (see esp. John R. Searle, "Las Meninas and the Paradoxes of Pictorial Representation," *Critical Inquiry* 6 [Spring 1980]: 477–88, together with the response of Joel Snyder and Ted Cohen, "Reflexions on *Las Meninas*: Paradox Lost," ibid., 7 [Winter 1980]: 429–47). But while they founder on the lack of valid internal distinction between particular and local effects that have been designated by such terms from antique literary theory on, and a more general and encompassing usage, the basic difference in the way in which one would use these terms for, say, works of Michelangelo and of Gauguin remains reasonably clear.

29. See Harriet and Sidney Janis, "Marcel Duchamp, Anti-artist," *View* (New York), ser. 5, no. 1 (March 1945), reprinted in *Marcel Duchamp in Perspective*, ed. Joseph Masheck (Englewood Cliffs, N.J., 1967), pp. 35–36 (quoting Duchamp).

30. See Arturo Schwarz, *The Complete Works of Marcel Duchamp* (New York, 1969), p. 470, under no. 252, *The Corkscrew's Shadow*.

31. See the account given by Pierre Cabanne, *Entretiens avec Marcel Duchamp* (Paris, 1967), trans. as *Dialogues with Marcel Duchamp* (New York, 1971), pp. 64–65.

32. Schwarz, *Works of Duchamp*, no. 332, measuring 4 x 5-1/2 x 5 inches

33. In a recent review of Gombrich's *The Image and the Eye: Further Studies in the Psychology of Pictorial Representation*, Rosalind Krauss makes a point that, in the context of her earlier account of Duchamp ("Notes on the Index: Seventies Art in America, Pt. I," *October* 3 [1977]: 68–81) is valuable here. She wrote then: "The photograph is thus a type of icon . . . which bears an indexical relationship to its object," meaning that, as distinct from symbols, "indexes establish their meaning along the axis of a physical relationship to their referents. They are the marks or traces of a particular cause and that cause is the thing to which they refer . . . " (pp. 75, 70). In the review (*Raritan* 2, no. 2 [Fall 1982]: 75–86), returning to the "ambiguous" duck-rabbit illustration now famous from its use in *Art and Illusion*, she denies Gombrich's claim that the figure is to be seen either as a rabbit or, alternatively, as a duck. "Free at last, it functions as the signifier of neither duck nor rabbit, but the unified concept *ambiguity*, thus taking a special place in that historical period for which the ambiguous is held most dear" (p. 86). The defect of Gombrich's account, on her analysis, is the reading of contemporary visual materials like advertisements and photographs in terms that are only applicable to the old master art of earlier times. For example, he elsewhere contrasts a Dali in which that artist's "way of letting each form represent several things at the same time may focus our attention on the many possible meanings of each colour and form" with the way that traditional pictures usually had each form and color "signify only one thing in nature" (*The Story of Art* [1950], p. 443). For us, this interesting dispute between Krauss and Gombrich involves not just issues of historical questions about the changing ways in which images get analyzed, but

134

also that ambiguity in the notion of truth itself on which we have focused.

34. The text in one case even goes as far as to speak of "creamy soft lathers on pale padded bottoms," and goes on to cite "pure temptation" in consumable forms, "the Milk Shake and the Hot Fudge Sundae," which seems to match up with the contrasting forms of invitingness of the young women.

35. For an interesting discussion of the larger role of the "made-up" elements in the blending of journalism and fiction practiced by some current writers (Truman Capote, Tom Wolfe, Norman Mailer), see John Hersey, "The Legend on the License," *Yale Review* 70, no. 1 (Oct. 1980): 1–25.

36. Rodney Needham, in *Belief, Language and Experience* (Oxford, 1972), discusses this question as an anthropologist and provides some evidence on the subject.

37. Stanley Fish, *Is There a Text in This Class? The Authority of Interpretive Communities* (Cambridge, Mass. and London, 1980), is to be found disagreeing, in chap. 11 (which was first publ. 1978), with John Searle (*Speech Acts* [Cambridge, 1969]) over the idea that one can speak of a "normal" context of utterance for a speech act, and he similarly rejects earlier in the essay (pp. 284–92) the notion that a sentence has a literal meaning in the sense of "some irreducible content that survives the sea change of situations." Searle meanwhile, it should be noted ("Literal meaning," *Erkenntnis* 13, no. 1 [July 1978]: 207–23, reprinted in his *Expression and Meaning: Studies in the Theory of Speech Acts* [Cambridge, 1979], chap. 5) has moved to a closely similar view, arguing that no statements have a literal meaning without a context of specification (see esp. pp. 125, 131–32). Fish's leading example of the different possible interpretations that might be given to the words *private members only* (pp. 274–77), is in fact one that confuses the implications that these words on a door conventionally carry, and the metaphorical suggestions that they might be taken to carry in some other context (such as on a classroom blackboard). The necessary distinction here is one also brought out by Alexander Nehamas, "The Postulated Author: Critical Monism as a Regulatory Ideal," *Critical Inquiry* 8, no. 1 (Autumn 1981): 133–49, when he writes that "the locutionary content of a sentence does not itself determine what illocution that sentence is being used to perform in a particular case," and, correspondingly, though the "central core" or fundamental level of meaning for a text determined by the rules of language "limits the overall interpretation of a text, it does not exhaust its meaning" (p. 138).

38. See David Carrier, "Berger on the Female Nude" (from the review essay, "John Berger as Critic," written jointly with Mark Roskill), *Studies in Visual Communication* 7, no. 2 (Spring 1981): 79, for the use of this as an example of the directly erotic power of a painting, that can only be understood at the same time in the context of traditional mythology.

39. For the inherence of such a quality in the associations used in advertising, see also Erving Goffman, *Gender Advertisements* (New York, 1979), where

the terms "behavioral choreography" and "stereotypical epitomization" are applied to group images (pp. 8, 26). Sir Ernst Gombrich, "Image and Code: Scope and Limits of Pictorialism in Visual Representation," in *Image and Code*, ed. W. Steiner (Ann Arbor, Mich., 1981), has recently reproduced some "advertisements" (figs. 9–14) in which "impossible" (rather than illogical) combinations of elements are brought together for humorous or arresting purposes; this is a form of imagery—equally adaptable to the medium of photography (e.g., producing a "trick" image of a head with three ears)— which has its own pictorial and illustrational tradition behind it.

40. Charles Henry Hart, *Browere's Life-Masks of Great Americans* (New York, 1899), chap. 3, p. 27. The entry under no. 17, James Monroe, offers the interesting further argument that a death mask cannot preserve the "spirit and expression" in the same way, because the ligaments become relaxed after death, bones lose their exact position (the slight weight of the plaster may increase this change), and the mask may reproduce "peculiarities of formation which may not be observable superficially" as the features settle. The life mask of William Blake has been chosen as illustration here because it was made by a phrenologist, and because Blake's wife disliked it on the supposition that it showed pain in the way we have mentioned.

41. Pure landscape and genre subjects, which have been left to one side in our account, may embody a scientific or an ethnological kind of truth (as in the rendering of light-color and atmosphere in one case, and the social and domestic customs of a class or people in the other), but the use of the word *truth* to that effect diverges in the nineteenth century from the tendency to posit a sensible idea of truth, based on practical knowledge and experience, and to make that the implied criterion in these heavily stereotyped branches of imagery, as in the comment of Stendhal on Constable cited in chap. 1, n. 2.

42. Vladimir Nabokov, *Ada or Ardor: A Family Chronicle* (New York, 1965), p. 146.

43. See Mark Roskill and Roger Baldwin, "André Kertesz's 'Chez Mondrian'," *Arts* 51, no. 5 (Jan. 1977): 106–7, for a fuller discussion, from which these remarks are excerpted.

*Chapter Three*
*Visual Lying: On the Notion of Falsehood*
*in Art and Photography*

1. *Nuns and Soldiers* (London and New York, 1980), p. 29. The context of this line, spoken by one of the characters, is a visit to the National Gallery in London, and the specific reference is to the works by Titian, Poussin, and such, which are being looked at, but the comment can also be taken as a philosophical leitmotif for the novel as a whole—as suggested by Mary Matthews who supplied this text.

2. Sissela Bok, *Lying: Moral Choice in Public and Private Life* (New York, 1978); the quotations are from p. 242.

3. Hans Sedlmayr, "Die 'Macchia' Bruegels," *Jahrbuch der Kunsthistorisches Sammlungen in Wien* 8 (1934): 137–59.

4. Hans Sedlmayr, *Verlust der Mitte: Das bildende Kunst des 19 and 20 Jahrhunderts als Symptom und Symbol der Zeit* (Salzburg, 1951), trans. by Brian Battershaw as *Art in Crisis* (London, 1958).

5. Cf. Heinrich Schwarz, "The Mirror of the Artist and the Mirror of the Devout: Observations on Some Paintings, Drawings and Prints of the 15th Century," in *Studies in the History of Art Dedicated to William A. Suida on his Eightieth Birthday* (London, 1959), pp. 90–105, citing four paintings of around 1500 of *St. Luke Painting the Virgin* from which such an implication can be drawn, and also Schwarz, "The Mirror in Art," *Art Quarterly* 15 (1952): 99.

6. Roger Fry, "Claude," *Burlington Magazine* 11 (1907): 267–98 (reprinted in his *Vision and Design* [1920; rev. ed., Harmondsworth, 1937], pp. 181–89).

7. See Marcel Rothlisberger, *Claude Lorrain: The Drawings*, 2 vols. (Berkeley, Calif., 1968), 1: 10–11, and also p. 7 (on the total picture now provided of Claude's drawings) and pp. 18–19 (comments on Sandrart's text).

8. Arnold Hauser, *The Social History of Art*, 2 vols. (New York, 1951), vol. 2, pt. 6, chap. 1, "The Dissolution of Courtly Art," esp. p. 521.

9. Those wishing to debate this point further, as it applies to fifteenth- to seventeenth-century art, both Italian and Northern, may wish to consider the creation of "dream worlds" made up of disparate and mutually incompatible elements (as in Marcantonio Raimondis's *Dream of Raphael*, or Bosch); the idea of disguise and deceit as represented in the form of figures with masks (Bronzino, Bruegel); and the depiction of the model as acting out a specific role assigned by the artist (as in Caravaggio's early paintings of boys and Vermeer's *Artist in the Studio*). Grateful thanks are owed to Craig Harbison and Iris Cheney for much helpful discussion in this connection.

10. The art educator and critic John Canaday's book *Mainstreams of Modern Art* (New York, 1951), has become the locus classicus for the expression of this view. See chap. 5, "The Salon at Mid-Century," esp. pp. 144–45 (on Meissonier), 152, 154 (on Gérôme and Bougereau), 151 (on Winterhalter).

11. See, for instance, the very recent article by George Lakoff and Mark Johnson, "Conceptual Metaphor in Everyday Language," *Journal of Philosophy* 77, no. 8 (August 1980): pp. 453–86, along with their book *Metaphors We Live By* (Chicago, 1980), and also Sol Worth, "Seeing Metaphor as Caricature," *New Literary History* 6 (1974), issue on Metaphor, p. 197 (reprinted in his *Studying Visual Communication*, ed. Larry Gross [Philadelphia, 1981], pp. 149–50).

12. Cf. Mark Roskill's discussion of this, with examples from the work of Rodin and Soutine, in "Looking Across to Literary Criticism" (contribution to a symposium), *Arts* 45 (June 1971): 16–18.

13. E. H. Gombrich, *The Story of Art* (London, 1950), pp. 434, 439, 443.

14. E. H. Gombrich, *Art and Illusion: A Study in the Psychology of Pictorial Representation*, A. W. Mellon Lectures in the Fine Arts, 1956 (New York, 1960), pp. 244 and fig. 210, 266 n. (Escher); p. 200 and fig. 246; p. 234 and fig. 194 (chimney); p. 345. See also his essay "The Mask and the Face: The Perception of Physiognomic Likeness in Life and Art," A. and F. B. Thalheimer Lecture, 1970, in E. H. Gombrich, Julian Hochberg, and Max Black, *Art, Perception and Reality* (Baltimore and London, 1972), pp. 1–46. More recent discussions of photography by him are cited in n. 20 below.

15. Cf. Gombrich's own reply on this subject, "The Sense of Order: An Exchange," *New York Review of Books*, Sept. 27, 1979, pp. 60–61.

16. John Berger et al., *Ways of Seeing* (London, 1972), pp. 52, 55–57, 139–42, 143–48; based on a BBC television series with the same title.

17. John Berger, *Permanent Red: Essays in Seeing* (London, 1960), pp. 64–65, 131; "Magritte and the Impossible" (1969), reprinted in Berger, *About Looking* (New York, 1980), pp. 155, 160.

18. Helmut Gernsheim, *Creative Photography: Aesthetic Trends 1839–1960* (New York, 1960), chap. 7, "'Fine Art' Photography" (the locus classicus for the expression of this view), and p. 89.

19. Berger, *About Looking*, pp. 29–32, 44–45, 62.

20. Roland Barthes, "Le message photographique" ( *Communications* 1 [1961]), trans. as "The Photographer's Message" in his *Image, Music, Text* (New York, 1977). For the highly personal version of a structuralist viewpoint that he moved to at the end of his life, see his *La chambre claire: note sur la photographie* (Paris, 1980), trans. as *Camera Lucida* (New York, 1980), in which he revised his influential earlier essay, "Rhétorique de l'image" (*Communicatons* 4 [1964]).

Pierre Bourdieu et al, *Un art moyen: Essai sur les usages sociaux de la photographie* (Paris, 1965). See also Jean A. Keim, *La photographie et l'homme: sociologie et psychologie de la photographie* (Tournai, 1973).

Susan Sontag, *On Photography* (New York, 1978), of which there is a most perceptive review by Maren Stange, *New Boston Review*, Spring 1978, p. 12.

Cf. also André Bazin, "On the Ontology of the Photographic Image" (from his *Problèmes de la peinture* [1945]), in *What is Cinema?* ed. and trans. Hugh Gray, 2 vols. (Berkeley and Los Angeles, 1967), 1: 9–22; William Ivins, Jr., *Prints and Visual Communications* (London and Cambridge, Mass., 1953), chaps. 5–7, discussed further by Estelle Jussim, *Visual Communication and the Graphic Arts* (New York and London, 1974); John Szarkowski, "Another Kind of Seeing," *New York Times Magazine*, April 13, 1975, pp. 16, 65–68; Joel Snyder and Neil Walsh Allen, "Photography, Vision and Representation,"

*Critical Inquiry* 2, no. 1 (Autumn 1975): 143–70 (which is a reply to Rudolf Arnheim, "On the Nature of Photography," ibid. 1 [Sept. 1974]).

Walter Benjamin's ideas on photography, set out in gnomic essay form in his *Illuminations*, trans. Hannah Arendt (New York, 1968) and *Angelus Novus*, trans. in *Screen* 13, no. 1 (Spring 1972): 5–26, are not broad enough in scope to be helpful; but they have been adopted wholesale by V. Kahmen, *Photographie als Kunst* (Tubingen, 1973), trans. as *Art History of Photography* (New York, 1974). John Berger has an essay using Benjamin (cited in chap. 2, n. 12) that appears in his *Another Way of Telling* (New York, 1982), written in collaboration with Jean Mohr. Recent writings by Gombrich on photography are his introduction to the exhibition catalogue "Henri Cartier-Bresson," Edinburgh (Scottish Arts Council) and Victoria and Albert Museum, London, 1978, and his essay "Standards of Truth: The Arrested Image and the Moving Eye," *Critical Inquiry* 7, no. 2 (Winter 1980): 237–74 (reprinted in *The Language of Images*, ed. W. J. T. Mitchell [Chicago, 1980], pp. 181–217, and in Gombrich, *The Image and the Eye: Further Studies in the Psychology of Pictorial Representation* [Oxford and Ithaca, N.Y., 1980], pp. 244–77), where he contrasts photographs that offer information about the world "out there" with more recent ones that, he claims, offer evocations that appeal to subjective visual experience. Since some of the most promising contributions so far toward the needed framework for discussing photography have come from a sociological and/or anthropological viewpoint, mention should be made particularly of Dan Sperber's book, *Le symbolisme en général* (Paris, 1974), trans. as *Rethinking Symbolism* (Cambridge, 1975), from which a starting point and sense of support have come for the argument hereafter, though the terms adopted and the application to photography are our own; and also Larry Gross, "Sol Worth and the Study of Visual Communication," *Studies in Visual Communication* 6, no. 3 (Fall 1980): 2–19, which presents strong parallels to the account of verbal communication given by Barbara Herrnstein Smith, *On the Margins of Discourse: The Relation of Literature and Language* (Chicago, 1978), chap. 4, "In the Linguistic Marketplace."

21. *Camera Lucida*, p. 87.

22. A short look at any mail-order catalogue of the moment that uses graphics will give a good overview of literal and nonliteral images, coexisting in a case like this often side by side; but it will also give a sense of the many differing means, which we take up later, by which literal images can be converted into nonliteral ones.

23. Response to photographic images that have been processed through a computer—whether of the Mona Lisa or the moon surface—raise altogether different associations/feelings about trustworthiness. So far, however, they have only been publicized for specific functional or demonstrational purposes.

24. Cf. here Sperber's account of symbolic processing, *Rethinking Symbolism*, p. 119, from which we have adapted some of the formulation.

25. This is discussed by Barthes in his "Le message photographique," which deals mainly with press photography.

26. See Pete Daniel and Raymond Smock, *A Talent for Detail: The Photographs of Miss Frances Benjamin Johnston, 1889–1910* (New York, 1974), pp. 100–101.

27. See William Stott, *Documentary Expression and Thirties America* (New York, 1973), pp. 284–87; and James C. Curtin and Sheila Grannen, "Let Us Now Appraise Famous Photographers: Walker Evans and Documentary Photographs," *Winterthur Portfolio* 15, no. 1 (Spring 1980): 1–24.

28. For the circumstances of its creation and appearance in this form (it is demonstrably a montage combining two different views, but there were also witnesses to claim that the artist had actually performed such a leap earlier, without catchers—a very Duchamp-like situation), see Thomas McEvilley, "Yves Klein, Messenger of the Age of Space," *Artforum* 20, no. 5 (Jan. 1982): 38, 47–48, or the same material as presented by him in the exhibition catalogue "Yves Klein, 1928–1962: A Retrospective," Museum of Contemporary Art, Chicago; Guggenheim Museum, New York; and Centre Pompidou, Paris, Feb. 1982–May 1983 ("Yves Klein, Conquistador of the Void").

29. Although in a painting or a print spectatorial viewpoint may be similarly controlled, in the implications that it raises of involvement or distancing in regard to what is presented, the public will be as much (or more) interested in accoutrements and physical characteristics introduced by choice and volition of the artist as in the role itself.

30. Susan Sontag, "Fascinating Fascism," *New York Review of Books*, Feb. 6, 1975 (reprinted in her book of essays *Under the Sign of Saturn* [New York, 1980], pp. 78–108). The Riefenstahl book (New York, 1974) first appeared as *Die Nuba* (Munich, 1973).

31. See *Joseph Beuys: Life and Works*, ed. Gotz Adriani, Winifred Konnertz, and Karin Thomas; trans. from German by Patricia Lech (Woodbury, N.Y., 1979), p. 15, pl. 4. The credibility of the setting and the idea that a crashed plane should look like this and that Beuys should be standing beside it come into question here. Further photographs purporting to show the remains of the crashed plane appear in Caroline Tisdall, *Joseph Beuys*, exhibition catalogue, Guggenheim Museum, New York, 1979, p. 17.

32. See Robert Smithson, "Incidents of Mirror-Travel in the Yucatan," first published in *Artforum* 8, no. 1 (September 1969), reprinted in the *Writings of Robert Smithson: Essays with Illustrations*, ed. Nancy Holt (New York, 1979), pp. 94–103. See also the discussions of 1970 with Michael Heizer and Dennis Oppenheim reprinted there, citing their work alongside Smithson's and making reference to photography, pp. 171–78; and Gianfranco Gorgoni's photographs of the work of Beuys, Smithson, and Heizer, as they appear in *The New Avant-Garde: Issues for the Art of the Seventies*, text by Grégoire Muller

140

(New York, 1972), which Hugh Davies kindly drew to our attention.

33. Such art needs to be either experienced directly or described in detail for its implications to be fully brought out. There is no overall study to date of the uses of photography in question, but for recent and related comment on some of these uses, see Rosalind Krauss, "Notes on the Index: Seventies Art in America," pt. 1, *October* 3 (Spring 1977): 68–81; Craig Owens, "The Allegorical Impulse: Toward a Theory of Post-Modernism," pt. 2, ibid. 13 (Summer 1980): 59–80; and, more particularly, Douglas Crimp, "The Photographic Activity of Postmodernism," ibid. 15 (Winter 1980): 91–101 (discussing the work of Cindy Sherman, alongside that of Sherrie Levine and Richard Prince, and also performances by Jack Goldstein and Robert Longo, and using Walter Benjamin's concept of presence in a photograph becoming an absence). For Sherman's still more recent work, see her "Untitled Film Stills," in *Paris Review* 22( Winter 1981): 133–39. Particular thanks are owed to Anne Mochon for providing these and other references for the last part of the chapter and for much helpful discussion of this subject based on her knowledge and experience. The terms *metatruth* and *metafiction* are our own, but they relate interestingly to the use of *meta-irony* by Duchamp (cited p. 61 above).

34. See for example the work of Duane Michals and Lucas Samaras.

35. How this might affect other branches of photography than those considered in this chapter is suggestively brought out in two recent "Photography View" columns in the *New York Times*, where the idea of the camera as "an instrument of ultimate truth" embodied in the nature photographs of Charles Pratt comes to seem too hermetically self-sufficient and even falsifyingly self-complacent for a world in which "nature and man are assumed to be separate" (Andy Grundberg, June 27, 1982); and where the selection of historical photographs from a vast body of available historical material and their presentation without verbal comment, in Michael Lesey, *Bearing Witness: A Photographic Chronicle of American Life, 1880–1945*, is so much "one person's view of truth" that it threatens to play false to history, by seeming to render it meaningless (Gene Thornton, Jan. 2, 1983). See also Grundberg's "Seeing the World as Artificial" (on the work of Laurie Simmons), *New York Times*, March 27, 1983.

*Chapter Four*
*How to Analyze Truth and Falsity*
*in Visual Images: Some Concluding Suggestions*

1. "Decoding Symbolism," Stanton Lecture, Cambridge University, 1979 (ms. p. 9, from a copy kindly supplied by her).

2. In Schapiro, *Modern Art: 19th and 20th Centuries* (New York, 1978).

3. As Marian Hobson indicates in the introduction to her book *The Object of*

*Art:The Theory of Illusion in Eighteenth-Century France* (Cambridge, 1982), which deals with painting and with the other arts (the novel, theater, poetry, music) in parallel.

4. One of the virtues of Michael Podro's recent *The Critical Historians of Art* (New Haven and London, 1982) is that it makes this attempt.

5. See Putnam, *Reason, Truth and History* (Cambridge, 1981), p. 128.

6. Rorty, *The Consequences of Pragmatism* (Minneapolis, 1982).

7. Auerbach, *Mimesis*, trans. W. Trask (Garden City, N.Y., 1957), p. 492.

8. Jonathan Culler's *The Pursuit of Signs: Semiotics, Literature, Deconstruction* (Ithaca, N.Y., 1981), serves as a useful introduction in English to the history and theory of semiotic analysis, especially chap. 2, "In Pursuit of Signs" (first published in 1977). The term *semiotics* suggests itself as being the best and most appropriate one for the present consideration of visual images; *structuralism*, as Culler defines and illustrates its workings in the domain of literature, cannot be made to apply without modifications and qualifications of purpose to visual images, and *semiology* as a form of analysis rests on a basic conception of "signs"—most often units of independent verbal meaning—which equally (as briefly indicated in n. 22 to chap. 1) raises problems of transposition and analogy. As Vincent Descombes has pointed out very clearly (*Le même et l'autre* [Paris, 1977], trans. as *Modern French Philosophy* [Cambridge, 1980], chap. 3), the "structure," the workings of which one seeks to establish in such a connection—whether the subject of one's study be verbal, visual, or behavioral—must in principle be that of the "set" which is representatively exemplified in the cases that one deals with, not that of any particular text, representation, or institution. An adequate formulation for visual images may also have to pry itself free from excessive dependency on the earlier writings of Roland Barthes, which posit an analytical method that could bring out the "connotations" governing whole systems of behavior, life styles, and forms of imagery such as advertising or photography, and reveal the "meanings" derived from participation in the system: a view which Barthes recanted in his last writings.

9. The division of visual images into three sign-types originated by C. S. Peirce is retained here for explanatory convenience, but it is retained in an adaptation that shifts emphasis, in the application of the three terms, to the generative and transformative processes that are entailed.

10. Cf. Dan Sperber, *Rethinking Symbolism* (Cambridge, 1975), p. 119, highlighting two basic aspects of symbolic processing that he designates as "focalization" (a displacement of attention) and "evocation" (a search in the memory). The terms *excerption* and *condensation*, not used by him, have been chosen for the more particular ways in which they characterize what one meets with in the case of visual images; the idea of an "excerptive" process being suggested in part by the German term *Herauslösung*, which Christian Tumpel

introduced into studies of Rembrandt and his school, on a somewhat related basis.

11. Such were the complaints of the official British historians, as represented by Robert Rhodes James's letter to the *Times* (London), Dec. 19, 1981, regarding the way in which the Australian assault at The Nek was presented in its relation to the British landing at Suvla; and by the comment of Michael Howard claiming that the war itself was "carefully sanitized," to include "nothing . . . in the slightest degree nasty" (*Times Literary Supplement*, Dec. 18, 1981, p. 1464).

# Index

144

Performance art, 104–7, 108–9, 118
Perspectivism, 12–14
Play acting: by camera, 103–4; by
  subjects, 31–33, 49, 60–66, 86–88,
  136 n.9
Portraits, 17, 31–33, 47–50, 53–55,
  59, 72–73
Postmodernist art, 95, 108–9,
  140 n.33

Rauschenberg, Robert, *Factum I,
  Factum II*, 47; *48*
Relativism, xii, 12–13, 23, 27–28,
  66, 68–70, 123 n.18
Rembrandt van Ryn: portraits of
  models, 31, 128 n.1; *Self-Portrait*,
  43–47, 50; *45*
Renoir, Pierre Auguste, *Moulin de la
  Galette*, 73–75; *74*
Riefenstahl, Leni, 103–4; *104*

Salon painting, 88–90, 92, 127 n.38
Semiology, 123 n.18, 141 n.8
Seurat, Georges, *Sunday Afternoon
  on the Island of La Grande Jatte*,
  55–57, 131 n.23; *56*
Skepticism, x–xi, 12–14, 22–23, 68
Smithson, Robert, *Nine Mirror Displacements in the Yucatan*, 105–6,
  139–40 n.32; *106*
Structuralism, xi, xii, 12–13, 23,
  68–70, 124 n.22, 137–38 n.20,
  141 n.8

Toulouse-Lautrec, Henri de, *Loie
  Fuller*, 4, 11, 20; *5*
Truth: linguistic, vii–x, 12, 17–19,
  22, 107–9, 124–25 n.23,
  134 n.37; 136 n.11, 138 n.20; and
  literature, 13–14, 16–17, 66–70,
  114, 123 n.19, 134 n.35, 141 n.8;
  metatruth, 107, 140 n.33; philosophical theories of, ix, xiii–xiv,
  coherence theories, 6, 121–22 n.9,

correspondence theories, 4, 79,
  114–15, 121–22 n.9. *See also*
  Metaphor, Perspectivism, Relativism, Semiology, Skepticism, Structuralism, Truth of visual images
Truth of visual images, 3–28 passim;
  and appropriateness, 6–7; emblematic, 79; expression of period,
  21–22, 39–40, 73–75; historical
  relativism of, 23, 36–37, 68; narrative truth, 7–9, 24–27, 127–
  28 n.38; and play with truth, 39,
  51–76, 86–88, 98–109, 117–18,
  132 n.28; and producers' intentions, 3–4, 21, 58–59, 109; and relations of images, 10–11, 17–19;
  and reproduction of images, 10;
  and theater, 23–24, 28, 37,
  126 n.32; truth of implications,
  vii–viii, 31–40, 50–76; and truth of
  statements, vii–viii, 17–19, 31–32,
  60, 96

Veronese, Paolo, *Mars and Venus
  United by Love*, 71–72; *71*
Visual ambiguity, 63–66, 133 n.33
Visual images: of authors, 17; and
  false beliefs, 31, 58–59; in film,
  119–20; literal, ix–x, 15–16, 19,
  37–38, 61–63, 95–97, 117,
  123–24 n.20; literalizing, 100–
  103; literal representation by, 48;
  nonliteral, 72–73, 95–98; photographs compared with paintings,
  ix–x, 15, 27, 37–38, 50–51, 68,
  93–95, 127 n.37; photomontages,
  xi, 14; plausibility of, 33; popular,
  113; realism of, 122–23; on record
  jackets, 11, 17, 28, 88–89; theatricalizing, 103–4; trick photographs, 101–3; of women, x,
  31–39, 64–66, 92–93. *See also* Advertisements, Death masks, Nudes,
  Portraits, Salon painting

Photographic sources and credits

1   Deutsche Fototek, Dresden

3   Space Photographs, Bladenburg, Maryland

7   Istituto Centrale del Restauro, Rome

8, 10, 19   Réunion des Musées Nationaux

27   Réunion des Musées Nationaux © SPADEM, Paris/VAGA,
New York 1983

18   Leo Castelli Gallery, New York (Robert Rauschenberg © 1983)

39   Estate of Robert Smithson, courtesy John Weber Gallery,
New York

40   Metro Pictures, New York

Other photographs have been provided by the museums,
authors, and owners whose names are furnished with the
illustration.